▶ Decoding Strategies

Decoding B2   **Student Book**

Siegfried Engelmann • Linda Meyer • Linda Carnine
• Wesley Becker • Julie Eisele • Gary Johnson

SRA McGraw-Hill

Columbus, Ohio

A Division of The McGraw-Hill Companies

Table of Contents

PHOTO CREDITS
Cover Photo: KS Studios

SRA/McGraw-Hill

A Division of The McGraw·Hill Companies

2002 Imprint
Copyright © 1999 by SRA/McGraw-Hill.

Send all inquiries to:
SRA/McGraw-Hill
8787 Orion Place
Columbus, OH 43240-4027

Printed in the United States of America.

ISBN 0-02-674786-3

8 9 VHJ 04 03 02 01

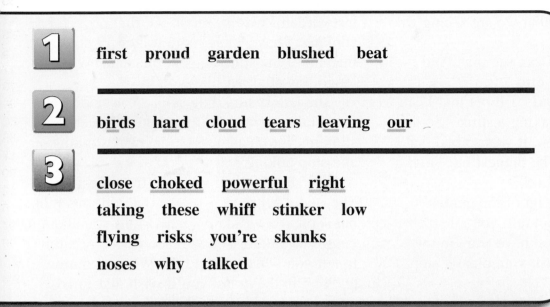

1 first proud garden blushed beat

2 birds hard cloud tears leaving our

3 close choked powerful right
taking these whiff stinker low
flying risks you're skunks
noses why talked

Five Stink Bugs Have a Contest

There were five stink bugs that lived in a garden. Stink bugs are proud if they can make a big stink. The biggest stink bug in the garden was very proud. She said, "This is how to make a stink." And she made a big stink that you could smell on the other side of the garden.

The fattest stink bug said, "If you think that her stink is so hot, look at what I can do." The fattest bug gave out with a smell that filled the air for three blocks.

The other bugs held their noses. They said, "That was as good a stink as we have smelled for some time."

[1]

The next stink bug had a striped back. He said, "If a bug has stripes on its back, it has the best stinker. Here I go." And there he went.

A stink came from him and fell like a cloud on the other bugs. They rubbed their eyes. They said, "If the air does not clear soon, we will pass out."

A bird was flying over the garden. She looked at the stink bugs in the garden and said, "What are you bugs doing? Don't you think that you'd better stop stinking? Remember there are others who have to smell your stink too."

[1]

"Stop talking," the striped stink bug said to the bird. "Can't you see that we are seeing who has the best stinker?"

The bird said, "Yes, I can see that. And I can smell that, too." The bird left.

The next stink bug said, "I'll bet that I can beat the rest of you in making a stink." So that bug began to make a stink. It was so bad that the other bugs choked. The biggest bug said, "Ugh! That was some stink!"

A rabbit at the other end of the garden called out, "So far as I can tell, you all smell the same. And that's bad. I have tears in my eyes. I cannot see. So I ask you, please, stop stinking."

[2]

"Stop talking," the biggest bug said to the rabbit. "We can't take time from our stink meet to talk to you. We are in the middle of something big."

The last stink bug was the smallest of all. She had spots on her back. She said, "Now that the rest of you are done, let me tell you about the stink that I'll make. Don't come too close when I begin stinking, or you will get so bent out of shape that you will never be the same. Nobody can stand the smell that I make."

[1]

The smallest stink bug kept talking, "In the last garden I was at, I took the first prize for stinking. I have taken more prizes for stinking than all of the stink bugs in this land. When I let go, my stink will lay you low."

The fattest stink bug said, "You're doing a lot of talking, but you're not doing much stinking. If you came to stink, start stinking and stop talking."

The smallest bug stared at the fattest bug. She said, "All right, I'll give out with my stink, but soon you will know why I told you about it before I let it go. You will see why I took time to tell you what it would do. When you are choking in the grass, you'll wish that I had made you leave the garden."

[2]

The striped bug said, "I'm not taking any risks. Any bug who talks like that must have some kind of stinker." So the striped bug left.

The little bug kept talking. She said, "One time, I made a stink that was so powerful it turned all the grass brown. I'll bet that I can beat ten skunks in a stinking contest."

The fattest bug said, "I came here for a stinking meet, not a talking meet. I'm leaving." And he did. The little bug kept talking. Soon another bug left.

[1]

1 call high waiting fort salt night forest

2 about breathed third bald
card fainting feared smallest

3 laugh burn straight die
wouldn't choke bet
deeply our afraid stinks

4 # The Little Bug Wins the Meet

There was a contest in the garden. Five stink bugs were trying to see who had the best stinker. All of the bugs but one had shown off their best stink. Now that bug began telling the others how good she was at stinking. She talked and talked. The other bugs began to leave. Now only the biggest bug was left.

The little bug with spots said, "If you wish, I will give you a very small stink. My smallest stink will choke you up for three hours. Would you like me to do that? Or would you like me to give the stink of stinks?"

[1]

"I'm getting tired of waiting," the biggest bug said. "No stink can be as good as you say your stink is."

The little bug said, "Then you're set for my stink? Breathe in deeply and hold in the air, for here it comes."

"No, wait," the biggest bug said. "Maybe I'd better go to the other side of the garden. I'll stand there, and I'll be able to get a better whiff of your stink."

The biggest bug was afraid. She feared that the smell would do her in. So she went to the other side of the garden.

[1]

The little bug asked, "Have you taken a big gulp of air?"

"Yes," the biggest bug said.

"Are your eyes closed?"

"Why should I close my eyes?" the biggest bug asked.

"My stink will burn your eyes so badly that you will not see straight for three days. My stink is so powerful that even bats get sore eyes when I turn on my stinker."

The biggest bug closed her eyes and breathed in deeply. Then she said, "I'm all set."

The little bug asked, "Are you grabbing onto something? Nobody can stand up when my stink reaches them. First it hits them so hard that they fall down. Then it knocks the air from them. And when it has done that, my stink chokes them up. But most bugs don't die from the smell. They are just sick for weeks."

[2]

The biggest bug said, "Wait. I'm not ready. I think I'll back up a little more."

"Tell me when you're ready," the little bug said. "I'll count to ten and then I'll turn on my stinker."

"All right," the biggest bug said, and that bug began to run. She ran so fast that the grass bent down as she went past. She ran up the hill on the other side of the garden. She didn't turn back. She didn't call to the bug. She just ran.

The little bug said, "That big stink bug can really run." Then the little bug began to laugh. That bug laughed so loud that a bird came to see who was making all the loud sounds.

[2]

"Why are you laughing so hard?" the bird asked.

Soon the bug stopped laughing. The bug said, "I'm laughing because I got rid of all those stink bugs."

"I'm glad of that," the bird said. "Where there are stink bugs, there is a lot of stink. I hate stink bugs."

"Me, too," said the little bug.

"Why should you hate stink bugs? You're one of them."

The little bug said, "I'm not one of them. I would never make a stink."

"Why wouldn't you make a stink?" the bird asked.

The little bug went, "Ho, ho." Then she said, "Because I am a lady bug."

[2]

1 each fold coach would

2 raised thirteen greenhouse smaller
blushed started always breed swing

3 studied botany skim basket
checks pond clod tried

4 fellow blade hang fifteen
lonely dribble block grow
school nothing skipping shy
stared stayed flowers grown
Patty along laugh burn

Lonely Art

Art was a farm boy. He talked like a farm boy. He walked like a farm boy. And when he was thirteen years old, he began to grow. When he was fifteen years old, he was taller than any other kid. His arms seemed too long. He looked like a long blade of grass.

After school, he didn't hang out with the other kids in his class. He went home to work on the farm. The other kids in his class said, "Art's a loner. He never hangs out with us." They didn't know that Art was shy.

[1]

A teacher in the school told Art that he should go out for basketball. And Art did. But he hadn't played basketball before. And he wasn't any good. He couldn't shoot the ball. He couldn't block shots. He couldn't dribble the ball.

The coach said, "Art, this game is too hard for you. Why don't you try out for another sport?"

But Art didn't try another sport. After school, he went down to the pond near his farm house. He skipped stones on the pond. He said to himself, "I just wish there were a stone-skipping team. I'd be the champ of that team."

[1]

Art could skip stones across the water like nothing you have ever seen. He could make the stones turn to the left or turn to the right. He could make them skip way up into the air. Or he could make them skim along the water. And if he took a big swing, he could make a stone skip almost to the other side of the pond.

But there was no stone-skipping team, and Art didn't have much fun in school that fall. He felt like a big clod. He felt that the other kids had a lot of fun, but he didn't fit into their plans. Art would smile and try to talk with them. But he didn't know what to talk about and they didn't seem to want to talk.

[2]

Then, in the winter, things were different. Patty came to Art's school. She was in two of Art's classes. One class was botany. Art tried to think of botany when he sat in that class, but Patty sat right in front of him. And every time he looked at Patty, he stopped thinking about botany and started to think about Patty.

One of the things they studied in botany was flowers. Art raised roses in his dad's greenhouse. So Art took some roses to school one day. He was going to show them to the class. One of them was a breed that Art's dad had grown.

[1]

Some of the boys saw Art going to class with the roses. "What are you going to do with those flowers, Art? Give them to Patty?"

In class, Art showed the roses to the teacher and the other kids. The teacher asked Art to tell about growing roses. So Art did. But he didn't give a very good talk. He kept looking at Patty.

When the class was over, Patty came up to him. She said, "That was a very good talk, Art." She had never said much to Art before, and Art felt funny talking to her. All of the other kids were looking at him.

[2]

Patty said, "Those are very pretty roses. What are you going to do with them?"

"I don't know," Art said.

"May I have one of them?" she asked.

Art blushed. "Yes, you can, Patty," he said. His cheeks felt hot. He gave her the biggest, reddest rose.

"Thanks a lot, Art," she said. "See you later." She walked from the room.

Then Tim came up. He stuck his finger in his mouth and said, "Say there, you big fellow. Can I have one of those roses, too? How about it, Big Boy?" He winked at Art.

[1]

1
raising blush starting couldn't
baseball night greenhouse
team tallest corner sailed coach

2
guy attention popular head friend
pitcher motorcycle catcher idea

3
staring laughing doesn't
Jackson trying isn't throw
players lesson crowd
Mark couldn't football

The Baseball Lot

Art was having a bad time in school. The kids didn't talk with him, and he didn't know what to say to them. After school, Art would go to the pond to skip stones. And as he skipped them, he said the things he would like to say to Patty.

"Patty," he said to himself one day, "I want you to be my girl friend." He skipped a stone and looked at it as it sailed almost to the other side of the pond. Then he said, "No, I will never say anything like that to Patty. I would just blush, and I wouldn't be able to say anything."

[1]

After school one day, Art saw Patty standing on the corner near school. He walked up to her. "Hi, Art," she said.

"Hi," he said. He breathed in deeply and said, "Can I walk with you?"

She smiled and said, "I'm waiting for somebody, Art. Sorry."

"That's okay," Art said, and he began to walk down the street. He looked back from time to time. When he was about a block away, he saw Mark Jackson walk up to Patty and begin to walk with her.

The next day, one of the kids told him that Mark Jackson was Patty's boy friend. Mark was one of the most popular boys in school and also one of the smartest.

[1]

Later that day, Art went to the pond and skipped stones. The pond was starting to freeze, and the air was cold.

"I wish I were a big football player," Art said to himself. He tossed a stone as far as he could. It went all the way to the other side of the pond. Art smiled. He had never skipped a stone that far before.

Then winter came. The winter seemed very long to Art.

But at last spring came and the trees started to bud. Now it seemed that the kids paid even less attention to Art.

[1]

"Maybe everybody has other things to think about now," Art said to himself. And they did. Some of them had motorcycles. Some had bikes. Some had boats. Some had girl friends. And some went out for baseball.

The baseball team worked out on a lot near the school. Art passed the lot every day. Sometimes he looked at the team before he went to the pond to skip stones or to the greenhouse to help his dad with the roses.

One day, Art stopped on his way home. He was standing next to a boy named Bart. "Hi, Art," Bart said. "Take a look at this pitcher they've got. He can make that ball buzz." So Art took a look.

[2]

The pitcher seemed to wave his arm around. Then he tossed the ball and the catcher grabbed it. "Did you see that?" Bart said. "That ball went like a shot."

Art smiled. "Was he trying to make the ball go fast?" Art asked.

Bart stared at Art. "What do you mean, trying? He made that ball go so fast, it went like a shot."

Art shook his head. "That wasn't very fast at all," he said.

Bart folded his arms. "Can you throw it any faster?"

"Well, yes, I can. I can throw it a lot faster."

"That's a good one," Bart said, and started to laugh.

[1]

Then Bart called, "Hey, guys, we've got somebody who can throw the ball a lot faster than your pitcher. This guy can do it. He told me so."

A lot of other kids began to laugh. Then one of them yelled, "Hey, Coach! Why don't you let Art here show you how to throw the ball?"

Art looked at Bart. "Well, I can throw it faster than that," Art said.

"Okay, he's ready," Bart yelled. "He just told me so."

Everybody was laughing. Art didn't know what to say. He turned around and started to leave. But everybody was yelling, "Come on, Art. The coach wants you to give his boys a lesson. Come on."

[2]

1

leaned   catcher   mound
heaved   coach   outfit
whip   formed   could   stained

2

pitcher   asked   thinner   longer   head
just   blowing   moment   silent   we're
tomorrow   attention   hollered   crowd
friend   tossed   popular   stuffed

3

Art's Fast Ball

Art didn't know what to do. He wanted to leave, but everybody was yelling, "Come on, Art, show us how to pitch."

Some boys grabbed Art and started to lead him to the pitcher's mound. "Here he is, Coach," one of the boys hollered. "The star pitcher."

The coach walked up to Art. He said, "I don't know what this is all about, but we've got work to do out here. So throw the ball to the catcher. That will shut those guys up. Then get out of here."

"Okay," Art said. The coach handed him the ball.

[1]

Art turned to the coach and said, "Do I just try to throw it at the catcher as hard as I can?"

"That's right," the coach said. "Just throw it and get out of here."

The ball felt a little too big in Art's hand. It didn't seem to fit as well as a skipping stone.

He rubbed it a few times and got a good grip on it. Then he leaned back.

"Show them how—if you can," the boys yelled.

Art's long arm went back like a whip. Then it came forward like a whip. "Zip—pow." The catcher was on his seat.

[1]

Everybody was silent for a moment. Everything was still. Then somebody yelled, "Did you see that?"

"No," somebody else yelled. "Did he throw the ball yet?"

The catcher was blowing on his hand. He yelled, "Yes, I'll say he did!"

Then everybody began to say things like, "Wow!" They didn't yell the way they had before Art had pitched. They just looked at Art and said, "Wow!"

The coach said, "Let's see you do that again."

The catcher tossed the ball to Art. Everybody fell silent as Art leaned back. His arm went back like a whip. Then he heaved the ball. "Zip—pow." The catcher was on his seat again, shaking his hand and blowing into his mitt.

[2]

The coach said, "Wow! I don't think I've ever seen anybody throw a ball that hard."

Art said, "I have to go now." He started to walk from the pitcher's mound.

The coach said, "Art, I would like you to come out for baseball."

Art stopped. "You mean you want me to be on the baseball team?" he said.

"Yes," the coach said. "You have a real gift. You can become a fine pitcher."

Art wanted to yell, "Hot dog!" But he didn't. He nodded to the coach and said, "Okay, I'll come out tomorrow after school."

[1]

When Art reached the crowd on the side lines, everybody stepped back and made a path for him. Bart said, "Good job, Art."

Some of the other kids patted Art on the back. "Good pitching," they said.

But Art didn't sleep well that night. He kept thinking of pitching. He kept thinking about the way everybody had said, "Good job. Good pitching." He liked the way they said that. He liked the idea of being a star pitcher. The next day after school, he dressed in a baseball outfit.

[1]

Art said to one of the other boys on the team, "I've never worn an outfit like this before. It feels sort of funny." And it looked sort of funny. It seemed to make Art look taller than ever. It seemed to make his arms look longer and thinner.

The coach met Art near the pitcher's mound. The coach said, "Today I want to see everything you can do with a ball. When I see what you can't do, I'll know what we have to work on."

The catcher stuffed a big rag into his catcher's mitt so that Art's fast ball would not sting his hand so much.

[2]

1

which   leaned   couch   chest   high

right   heaved   cheered   mound

coach   should   beaten   jeered

2

curve   nobody   throw   went

want   friend   head   catch

different   pitches   plate   glared

crowd   mistake   batter   stuffed

showed   moment   whipped   skinny

3

The School Team

The coach wanted Art to show him everything he could do with a baseball. The catcher had stuffed a rag into his mitt so that Art's fast ball would not sting his hand so much.

"Let's see your fast ball," the coach said.

Art leaned back and—"Zip—pow." The catcher said, "Ow! That rag doesn't help very much." He tossed the ball back to Art.

Art dropped the ball. He picked it up and looked at the coach. The coach said, "Now can you make the ball curve?"

"What do you mean?" Art asked.

"Make the ball bend to the left or bend to the right."

"Oh, that," Art said. "Which way do you want me to make it bend?"

The coach stared at Art for a moment. Then he said, "Make it curve to the left."

"Okay," Art said.

[2]

Art leaned back and to the side. He said to himself, "This is just like making a stone curve to the left."

Art's arm whipped out to the side, and the ball went flying. It was going far to the right of the catcher. The catcher began to reach to the right, then the ball curved and hit him in the chest.

"Wow!" the coach said. "Who showed you how to do that?"

Art said, "Nobody." Then he told the coach about skipping stones on the pond every day.

[1]

The coach had Art throw a lot of balls that day. The coach had him throw balls that curved to the left and balls that curved to the right. The coach had him throw balls that dipped down just before they reached the catcher. He had Art throw balls that jumped up just before they reached the catcher.

The crowd on the side lines clapped after every ball Art heaved. And after every ten balls, the coach had a different catcher work with Art. After catching ten of his pitches, a catcher's hand was very sore.

[1]

Art worked out with the baseball team for three weeks. Then the team had its first game. The game was with a big school, West High School. West High was always a top team in the state. It had been the best team in the state three years before. Last year, it had been the third-best team in the state. Art's school had never beaten West High in a baseball game.

Art didn't sleep well before the game with West High. He kept thinking about the game. He wanted to do a good job. He hoped that he wouldn't throw a bad ball or make a mistake.

About two hundred kids from Art's school went to the game. About four hundred kids from West High came to cheer for West. They cheered and cheered. But they jeered as Art's team came out to start the game.

[2]

Art didn't like to hear the West High fans jeer at his team. He said to himself, "Why are they yelling those things? They've never seen us play." But the fans from West High kept on jeering and jeering.

West High was to bat first. So Art went to the pitcher's mound. The catcher tossed the ball to him, and Art dropped it.

"Ha, ha," a fan yelled. "He can't even catch the ball. Get a rake! Can you rake that ball in? Ho, ho."

The first batter was a big boy. He held the bat back and glared at Art. Art didn't like the way he glared, and Art tried not to look at the batter.

[1]

Art tried to think about pitching. He said to himself, "Don't throw the ball too high. Don't throw it too low. Don't throw it to the left of the plate. Don't throw it to the right of the plate."

Art was not thinking well. He was telling himself what he should not do. He should have been telling himself what he should do. He should have been saying, "Throw that ball right over the plate—right over it."

Art leaned back and gave the ball a heave. It went about nine feet over the catcher's mitt.

[1]

1 wouldn't reached coach
breathed started streak called

2 umpire cheering catch silent
fans who shouldn't

3 sting string Chuck stared
zing guy plate want
weren't doesn't isn't thrown
clapping shaking strike
taken state moment pitcher curve

4

Some Bad Pitches

Art had just thrown a bad ball. And the West High fans were cheering and clapping. "That's the way to pitch," they yelled.

The catcher tossed the ball back to Art, and Art dropped it. The West High fans cheered again. The fans from Art's school were silent.

Art picked up the ball. He breathed in and out three times. Then he said to himself, "Don't throw the ball too high. Don't throw the ball too high." Art was not thinking well again.

Art heaved the ball. It went like a streak. But it went about ten feet over the catcher's head. The catcher called time out and ran to the pitcher's mound.

[1]

The fans from West High cheered. "Get another pitcher," they yelled. "This one has had it."

The catcher said, "What's the matter, Art?"

"I don't know," Art said. His hand was shaking. "I can't make the ball go where I want it to go."

"Yes, you can, Art," the catcher said. "Just think about skipping stones. I'll hold out my mitt. You must throw that ball right into the mitt. Throw it just like you throw a stone. You can do it."

"I'll try," Art said.

The catcher jogged back and Art rubbed the ball around in his hand. He looked at the catcher's mitt, and he said to himself, "I'll throw that ball right into the mitt. I'll do it."

[1]

Now Art was thinking the right way. He leaned back. His arm whipped back. The ball came from his hand like a shot. "Zip—pow."

"Strike one," called the umpire.

The fans from Art's school cheered. The fans from West High mumbled. They said, "Was that a lucky toss?"

Art got ready for his next pitch. Everybody was silent. "Zip—pow." The catcher was down.

"Strike two," the umpire called.

The batter did not have a mean look now. He got set for the next pitch. He hadn't taken a swing at any of Art's pitches so far. Now he seemed set to take a swing at the next ball.

[1]

Art leaned back and—"Zip—pow." The catcher was down. And the batter began to swing after the ball had reached the catcher.

The fans from Art's school cheered and cheered. They jumped up and down. They hugged each other. They yelled, "Go to it, Art. Show them how to pitch."

The fans from West were very silent. Then some of them began to cheer, "Come on, Chuck. Get a hit off that pitcher."

Chuck was the next batter. He smiled as he walked up to the plate. The catcher jogged out to talk to Art. "This guy is good," the catcher said. "He is one of the best batters in the state. Don't give him anything he can hit."

[2]

So Art began to think to himself, "Don't give him anything he can hit. Don't give him a slow ball."

Art was not thinking right again. He was thinking about what he shouldn't do. He should have been thinking about what he should do. He was telling himself, "Don't throw a slow ball."

And what do you think Art did? He gave Chuck the biggest slow ball you have ever seen. And Chuck hit that ball right out of the park. The fans from West High jumped up and down. They hugged each other. They cheered and yelled. "A home run! A home run!"

[1]

The catcher jogged out to talk with Art again. The catcher said, "Art, that was a bad pitch. You can throw better than that. Just zing the ball in. Just think about skipping stones. You can do it."

The next batter came up. He was as tall as Art. The fans clapped and cheered when he got near the plate. "You are the best, Bob," one of them yelled.

Art remembered that Bob was the best batter on the West team. For a moment, Art began to think about the things that he should not do. Then he remembered what the catcher had said. He stared at the catcher's mitt, and he said to himself, "I'll just zing the ball right into that mitt."

[2]

1 started always whistle also
groaned almost reared wound

2 league pitcher couldn't two
different what went want

3 batters crowded handshakes
done tried tired stared star
care Tigers you'll doesn't
hadn't weren't winner ducked

4

Art Becomes a Star

The best batter on the West team was at the plate. Art was thinking about what the catcher had told him. Art reared back. He let the ball fly. "Zip—pow." The catcher was on his seat again.

"Strike one," the umpire called.

"You can do it, Bob," the West fans yelled.

Art got the ball again. He looked at the catcher's mitt. He reared back and let the ball fly. The ball started to go right at the batter. The batter ducked down. But almost before he could <u>move</u>, the ball curved and went right into the catcher's mitt.

"Strike two," the umpire called.

[1]

Again Art wound up and lct the ball fly. Bob took a big swing at it, but the ball was in the catcher's mitt before Bob began to swing.

"Strike three. You're out."

"Oh, no," the West High School fans groaned.

"Go, Art, go," the fans from Art's school yelled.

And Art went. He struck out every other batter in the game. Art did not do well when he tried to bat, but his team was the winner. They beat West High School 3 to 1.

Everybody from Art's school yelled and crowded around Art. They cheered. They patted him on the back. They gave him handshakes and smiles.

[1]

Art was so happy that he just sat down after all of the fans had left. He just sat and remembered the game. "Wow!" he said to himself. "I did it."

After that first game, things were different in school. The kids smiled at Art. They went out of their way to talk to him. Art felt a lot better about school. In fact, school was a lot of fun for Art now. He waved to the girls. He wasn't afraid to talk to girls. He didn't look down when he talked to them. He had done that before, but now he was Art the Star, the big pitcher.

[1]

And Art started to talk like a star. He began to act like a big star. He began to make fun of some of the other kids. He began to show off in front of the girls. He began to talk a lot more.

One day, he said to himself, "I want Patty to be my girl friend." So he walked up to her before class and said, "I'm not doing anything after school, so why don't we go for a walk?"

"No, thanks, Art," she said.

Art didn't know what to say then. Since he had become a pitching star, nobody said, "No, thanks, Art." They always said, "Yes, Art."

[2]

Art looked at Patty. "If that's the way you want it," he said, and walked down the hall. He started to whistle, just to show her that he didn't care if she went with him. But he felt bad. He liked Patty. But there was something in the way she talked that told Art, "I don't like you, Art."

Art was still thinking about Patty when somebody said, "Art. Art. The coach wants to see you right now."

"What does he want?" Art said.

The boy said, "I don't know, but it's something big."

[1]

Art went with the boy to see the coach. The coach said, "Art, there's going to be a big league baseball game in town. And before the game, they want some of the best high school pitchers to throw for the batters. I want you to throw for our school."

"Will I play in the game?" Art said.

"No," the coach said. "The Reds will be playing the Tigers. But before the game, you will pitch to some of the batters. Some of the other high schools are sending pitchers to do the same thing."

"That will be fun," Art said.

His coach said, "You'll be pitching to some of the best batters in baseball."

[2]

1 reared falling mound also waited
Art first speaker Garner hardest
league shouldn't almost always

2 worry voice exhibition stands
jogged filed done okay Hunt
shaking umpire James o'clock
started stared struck blinked

3
First Inning

Art was going to pitch to some big league players before the game on Sunday. His coach had told him that he would be pitching to some of the best batters in baseball.

The game was to start at one o'clock. Art was to begin pitching at noon. But at 12 o'clock there were not very many fans in the stands. Art walked to the pitcher's mound and picked up the ball. One of the players from the Tigers said, "Just throw fast balls. The batter will hit them into the left stands. Some of the fans will get free baseballs."

[1]

Art looked up at the left stands. About one hundred kids were up there. Some of them had baseball mitts. Art said, "Should I throw as hard as I can?"

"That's right," the player said. "Don't worry, the batter will hit the ball. You're pitching to James Hunt. He'll hit them, all right."

Art stared at the catcher's mitt. Then Art reared back and gave the ball the hardest heave he could give it. "Zip—pow!" The catcher was on his seat.

The player who was standing next to Art blinked and stared at Art. James Hunt looked at the catcher, and then he looked at Art. He blinked.

[1]

A fan yelled, "Did you see that? He shot that ball past James Hunt."

Another fan said, "Hunt is trying to make the kid look good. He'll belt the next ball."

But Hunt didn't have time to swing at the next ball. Before he began his swing, the catcher was on his seat again.

The catcher jogged out to the pitcher's mound. He said, "Hey kid, how do you do that? No pitcher has ever set me on my seat before. How do you do that?"

"I just throw hard," Art said.

And he did throw hard. He struck out James Hunt.

[1]

Art struck out other batters that day. Not many fans were in the park to see what Art had done, but every fan who was there was standing and clapping when Art left the pitcher's mound.

Art walked over to his coach and sat down. His coach had tears in his eyes. "You are the best," his coach said.

Then the coach for the Tigers walked up and sat down next to Art. He said, "Not many fans saw that. How would you like to pitch the first inning of the game? I think the fans should see what you can do. If you can strike out my Tigers the way you did, I'll bet you can strike out any player on the Reds."

"Okay," Art said, and he smiled.

[2]

Art was thinking, "Wow! I get to pitch to big league batters in a big league game."

The fans filed into the ball park, and Art waited. Then a voice came over the loud speaker. It said, "Today a boy from your town will pitch for the Tigers in the first inning. This boy is one of the best pitchers we have seen. His name is Art Garner."

The fans who had seen Art pitch before the game cheered and clapped. But the other fans didn't cheer.

[1]

One of the fans said, "We didn't come here to see kids play. We came to see the Reds and the Tigers."

Art walked to the mound. Then he looked up at the stands. He had never seen so many fans before. Suddenly he became afraid. He began to think about all of the things that he shouldn't do. "Don't throw the ball too high," he told himself.

The catcher tossed the ball to Art. And Art dropped it.

"Boooooo," yelled some of the fans. "Get that bum out of here." Art's hands felt cold, and his legs were shaking.

[2]

1

thousand   leaving   roared

waited   cheered   first   while

these   crash   leaned   right

proud   reared   afraid   sharp

2

records   nurse   turn   voice

shy   awake   worry   brakes

catcher's   dollars   hospital   mixed

driver   closer   strapped   showed   lonely

onto   two   alive   exhibition   fist

Things Take a Bad Turn

Art was standing on the pitcher's mound. His hands felt cold. The fans were yelling and booing because he had dropped the ball. The catcher yelled to him, "Come on, Art. Just zip it right in here." He pounded his fist into his mitt.

Art stared at that mitt. He stared and stared. "Look at that mitt," he told himself. Now he was thinking the right way again. He said, "I'm going to zip that ball right into the mitt." He leaned back and shot the ball at the catcher's mitt. The batter didn't have time to start his swing. The catcher was on his seat.

"Strike one," the umpire called.

[2]

The fans began to say, "Did you see that?"

Then the fans fell silent as Art reared back for his next pitch. "Zip—pow." Down went the catcher again.

"Strike two."

"Wow!" the fans yelled. Then they waited for Art's next pitch.

Again Art heaved the ball so hard that the batter did not have time to swing. "Strike three. You're out."

The fans clapped and cheered.

Art struck out the next batter with three pitches.

[1]

The last batter took a swing at Art's fast ball, but he missed it by a foot. As Art walked from the pitcher's mound, all of the fans were standing and clapping. The players from the Tigers and the Reds came out to shake hands with him.

Art felt proud. "Just think," he said to himself. "Last year, I was lonely and shy. But look at me now. I'm a star."

And he was a star. That night his dad showed him the paper. There was a story about Art and his pitching. "I'm proud of you, Art," his dad said.

[1]

People from the big league came over to talk to Art that night. A man from the Reds said that he would pay Art three hundred thousand dollars if Art left school and became a pitcher for the Reds. A woman from the Tigers told Art that she would give Art five hundred thousand dollars if Art played with the Tigers.

Art told them that he would have to think about leaving school.

Then some of Art's friends came over. They wanted to take Art to a party. Art asked his dad and mom, and they said that it was all right for him to go.

[1]

So Art got in the car. The driver zipped down the road from Art's farm. He went faster and faster. "This car is very fast," he told Art. Art did not like to go fast, but Art didn't want the other kids to think that he was afraid. So he didn't say anything.

The car roared down the road. Just then a truck turned onto the road. The driver hit the brakes. The car began to slide. It slid to the left, and then it went back to the right.

Nobody said a thing. They just watched the car come closer and closer to the truck. Closer. Closer.

[1]

When Art opened his eyes, he was looking at a green wall. He started to move. Then he saw that he was strapped into a bed. He felt a sharp pain in his arm. His arm was in a cast.

He looked around the room. A nurse was reading Art's records. When she saw that Art was awake, she put down his records and said, "Well, did you have a good sleep?"

"Where am I?" Art asked.

"You're in the hospital," the nurse said. "You are lucky to be alive."

"What happened?" Art said. Everything seemed mixed up.

"You were in a bad crash," she said. "A very bad crash."

[2]

1 nearly   should   outside
league   remember

2 curl   stairs   watched   scratched
itched   awake   sawed   broken
hospital   strapped   crying   alone

3 two   there's   chair   nurse
rubbed   cast   passed   records
else   wanted   tried   somewhere

4

He'll Never Pitch Again

Art was in the hospital. The nurse had just told him that he had been in a very bad crash. Art didn't remember the crash. He had a hard time thinking. His arm was in pain.

A doctor came into the room. The nurse said, "He's awake now."

The doctor walked up to Art's bed. "How do you feel?" she asked.

"I don't know," Art said. It was hard to think. "There's a pain in my right arm. Why is it in a cast?"

"Your arm is broken," the doctor said.

"That's the arm I throw with," Art said. "Is it bad? Will I be able to pitch soon?"

[1]

The doctor looked down. Then she stood up. "We should talk about this later," she said. "Right now, you should get some sleep."

"Tell me," Art said. "Will my arm be okay?"

The doctor rubbed her chin. "I'm afraid not," she said. "Your arm was broken in three spots. I don't think you'll ever be able to pitch again."

"No," Art said. "No, no." He began to sob. Art wanted to curl up into a little ball and hide. He wanted to be somewhere else. He wanted to believe that he was having a bad dream.

[1]

But Art's arm was in pain, and he kept hearing the words the doctor had said. "I don't think you'll ever be able to pitch again."

The doctor sat next to him on the bed. "I know that I can't say anything that will help," the doctor said. "But you must be brave. You feel as if your life is over, but it has just begun. I know."

Art looked up at the doctor. The doctor seemed to float in the tears that were coming from Art's eyes. He turned from the doctor.

[1]

Art had been in the hospital for nearly two weeks. A lot of kids had come to visit him, but he didn't see any of them. He told the doctor that he didn't want to see anybody but his mom and dad.

Patty came to the hospital one day, but Art didn't see her. He didn't want her to see him with his broken arm. He didn't want her to see him when he was in bed—all strapped up like a baby. Two of the other kids who were in the car with Art were in the hospital, but Art didn't want to see them.

On the day Art was to leave the hospital, the nurse asked if he would stop in and see his friends. "No," he said. "I want to go home." He wanted to be home. He wanted to be alone.

[1]

So he went home. His mom and dad came to the hospital to get him. His mom had been crying. His dad tried to be happy and tell jokes. But Art didn't say much. He sat in the car and watched the road as his dad drove home.

Art didn't go to school the next week. He sat. He didn't eat much or sleep much. He just sat. He sat on the stairs. He sat in a chair. He even went down and sat near the pond for a while. But that made him sad. He felt like skipping stones across the pond, but then he remembered that he would never throw well again. So he went back to the stairs and sat.

His arm was still in a cast, and it itched. But he couldn't scratch it. He tried to slap it, but it still itched. He scratched the outside of the cast, but that didn't help. He wanted to get rid of that cast.

[2]

Art wanted to go away from his home and his school. But he didn't know where to go. Two more weeks passed. Then it was time for the cast to come off. Art sat in the doctor's office and watched the doctor saw the cast. As the doctor sawed, Art said to himself, "I hope she doesn't saw my arm."

The cast came off in two parts. Art's arm felt funny. And it looked funny. It was thin. Art tried to bend it. It didn't bend. He tried again. It bent an inch or two.

The doctor said, "Take it easy. We'll start giving that arm some work in a few days, but don't try to bend it too much."

Art looked at his arm and said to himself, "So that's the arm that struck out three Reds in one inning. I can't even bend the arm."

[2]

1

dirt   fair   around   shame
weak   told   first   raised
hardly   always   about

2

heavy   exercise   friends   tried
skip   everybody   walked   front
month   care   believe   stared
sorry   moped   nodded   across
again   lonely   watched   stairs

Art Feels Sorry for Himself

The cast had been taken from Art's arm. And Art went back to school for the first time. Everybody tried to be friends. At least fifty kids told Art that they were sorry. But Art didn't say much. He just nodded and walked away. He went to his botany class and sat down.

Patty was sitting in front of him. She turned around and held up a big red rose. "Here's one that I raised," she said. "What do you think of it?"

Art said, "It's pretty. It's very pretty."

She smiled and turned back. Art didn't like the way she acted. Why didn't she say, "I'm sorry, Art"?

[1]

Patty didn't even seem to care. Art would never pitch again, and she didn't even care. After class, he walked up to her in the hall. He didn't know what he would say to her, but he wanted to talk. He wanted to hear her say that she was sorry. Art said, "I had my cast taken off."

"I see that," she said.

Art said, "The doctor said that I'll never pitch again."

She stared at him. Then she asked, "Do you believe that?"

"Yes," Art said. "She's a doctor. She should know."

Patty said, "Do you want to believe that you'll never pitch again?"

Art said, "No. I want to pitch."

[1]

Patty said, "Tell yourself that you can pitch, and you will pitch."

"No," Art said. "I don't think so. I can hardly bend my arm."

Patty said, "Maybe you don't want to bend your arm. Maybe you want to feel sorry for yourself."

Art felt his cheeks getting red. "I don't feel sorry for myself," he said, and walked away from her.

But Art did feel sorry for himself. He kept thinking about what a shame it was that he would never pitch again. He kept thinking about what a shame it was that his arm had been broken. And he liked to hear people say, "I'm sorry, Art." It was a lot better than being lonely.

[2]

Art didn't talk to Patty for a month. He moped around school, and he moped around the farm. He went to the doctor's office three times a week. The doctor had him do exercises for his arm.

Now Art could bend his arm almost all the way. But his arm was weak. It was so weak that he couldn't bend it when he held a heavy steel ball. The doctor told him that he should exercise his arm at home every day, but Art didn't feel like exercising. So his arm didn't get very strong.

[1]

A year passed, and his arm was still not strong. Some of the kids in school still talked about how good Art had been at pitching, but they didn't talk about him very much. And he didn't talk to them very much. He went to class and worked pretty hard, but not too hard. He helped his dad, and he did a fair job, but not a good job. And he still felt sorry for himself.

Then one day something happened. He was walking near the pond when he saw Patty riding a horse on the dirt road that went past the pond.

[1]

"Hi, Art," Patty called. She rode her horse next to him, stopped, and slid down from the horse.

She said, "What are you doing, skipping stones?"

"No," Art said. "I don't skip stones any more."

"Why not?" she asked.

"My arm," Art said. He felt himself getting mad. "I can't throw any more."

"Let's see you try," she said.

"No," he said. "I can't do it. At one time, I could skip a stone all the way across the pond. But that was when I had a good arm."

"Let's see how you do now," she said.

"No," Art said. "And I don't want to talk about it any more."

[2]

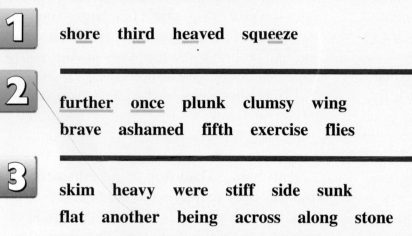

1 shore   third   heaved   squeeze

2 further   once   plunk   clumsy   wing
brave   ashamed   fifth   exercise   flies

3 skim   heavy   were   stiff   side   sunk
flat   another   being   across   along   stone
heavy   throwing   month   you'll

4
Patty Challenges Art

Patty was making Art mad. She was trying to get him to skip stones, but he didn't want to. He felt ashamed of himself.

Patty picked up a stone and smiled at him. She said, "If you're so bad at skipping stones, I'll bet I could beat you in a contest." She looked out over the pond. She pressed her lips. Then she tossed the stone. "Plunk," it went, and it sank. It didn't skip one time.

Art smiled. He said, "That was pretty bad."

She said, "I'll do better with this next stone." She picked up the stone, pressed her lips, and gave it a big toss. "Plunk."

[1]

Art laughed. Then he said, "You're not throwing the right way. You've got to get your arm down low, so that you can skim the stone across the water."

She picked up another stone and held her arm to her side. "Like this?" she asked.

"Sort of," Art said.

She made a face and tossed the stone. It skipped once. "There," she said. "Let's see you beat that."

Art laughed. "That wouldn't be very hard to beat." He picked up a stone. He leaned to the side. His arm felt stiff and funny when he went to whip it back. He tried to swing fast, but his arm seemed to move very slowly.

[1]

The stone skipped three times. It went further than Patty's stone. But the stone went less than a third of the way across the pond. Art was thinking to himself, "At one time I could skip a stone all the way across the pond."

Patty said, "That wasn't bad, but I'll bet I can beat it." She picked up a flat stone, bent to the side and let it fly. It went almost as far as Art's stone.

Art picked up a stone. "I'll make this one zip," he said. He bent to the side and let it fly. It went over a third of the way across the pond.

[1]

"That was good," Patty said. "Do you still think that you'll never pitch again?"

Art sat down on the shore of the pond. He didn't say anything for some time. Then he said, "At one time, I could skip a stone to the other side of the pond. Now I can't skip it anywhere near the other side."

Patty said, "But this is the first time you've thrown since you broke your arm. I'll bet you that within a month you'll be throwing a lot better. But you'll have to work at it every day."

[1]

Art said, "I once read that a bird with a broken wing never flies as high again."

Patty said, "Stop that. You're not a bird. And you don't have a broken wing. They fixed your arm. You just have to start being brave."

Art glared at her. "What do you mean? What makes you think I'm not brave?"

She grabbed his hand and gave it a squeeze. Then she said, "You don't like being you. You like being a pitcher. You like being a show-off. You like feeling sorry for yourself. But you don't like being Art Garner."

"That's not right," Art said. "I like being me."

[2]

Patty said, "Then stop being ashamed of yourself. Stop feeling sorry for yourself. Start working with yourself. You can be a pitcher if you want to. Maybe you won't be as good as you were. Maybe you'll have to work very hard. But if you set yourself to do it, you can do it."

For the next five days, Art kept thinking about what Patty had said. On the fifth day, he said to himself, "She's right. If I want to be a pitcher, I'm going to tell myself that I can do it. And then I will do it. I'll work until I do it."

On the next day, Art began to work. He began to exercise his arm. He began skipping stones on the pond again. At first he didn't try to throw them very hard, but each day he heaved a little harder.

[2]

1 tch

A	B
catch	pitcher
itch	hatch
match	catcher

2 nearly brains hardly
floated call heaved

3 glared slowly watch quit curve
tested timing foot umpire halfway
tried cried signaled gripped there's
facts locker inning fly try league
throwing swing coach once player
flashing smartest guy further blow

The Smartest Pitcher

Art became better, but it seemed very slow to him. After working for two months, Art could hardly throw a stone halfway across the pond. After six months, he could throw a stone a little more than halfway across the pond. After almost a year, he could make a stone skip pretty far—but not nearly as far as he had before he'd broken his arm.

Art went out for baseball the next spring. The first time he was on the pitcher's mound, the boys on the team yelled, "Come on, Art. Set that catcher on his seat."

[1]

Art heaved the ball just as hard as he could, but the catcher didn't go down. Art didn't have the same fast ball that he had before. The catcher didn't drop his mitt and blow on his hand after catching one of Art's fast balls.

Art wanted to quit the team after that first day. But when he was in the locker room, the coach came up to him. The coach sat down next to him and said, "Art, let's look at the facts. You don't have that flashing fast ball that you had before. But you can still become a good pitcher. You can make the ball curve. You can make the ball hop."

[1]

The coach said, "Before, you didn't have to make it curve or hop. You could just lay back and throw your fast ball. But now you're going to have to think. Before you broke your arm, you would win games with your arm. Now you're going to have to win games with your brains. Remember that—your brains."

In the first game Art's brain was tested. The test came in the first inning.

Art struck out the first batter with a fast ball. He started to think, "Maybe my fast ball has come back." So when the next batter stepped up to the plate, Art reared back and let fly with another fast ball.

"Crack." The batter hit the ball hard. It was a three-base hit.

[2]

Now Art was afraid. A player was on third base. There was one out. And Art didn't have a flashing fast ball that would strike out the other batters.

The catcher jogged out and said to Art, "Just make the old brain work, Art. You can strike this next guy out. Just throw the kind of pitch he's not looking for. Watch me. I'll give you some signals."

So Art watched the catcher. The catcher signaled for a slow curve. "No," Art said to himself. "He'll hit it out of the park." Then Art began to think, "Maybe he won't. Maybe he's looking for a very fast ball. Maybe a curve will throw his timing off and make him miss the ball."

[2]

So Art leaned back. He whipped his arm back just the way he did when he was throwing a fast ball. Then he let the ball go. But he didn't throw it fast. He floated it. The batter swung and missed the ball by a foot.

The batter gripped the bat and glared at Art. Art smiled at the catcher. That seemed to make the batter madder than ever. The catcher signaled for a ball outside the plate. Art heaved the ball.

The batter started to swing before he saw that the ball was pitched outside. He missed. Now the catcher called for a fast ball. Art heaved it as hard as he could. "Strike three," the umpire called.

[1]

Art struck out the next batter. In that game Art struck out 8 more batters, and Art's team was the winner.

And that's how Art got started years ago. Today he is a big league player. He's not as good as he would have been if he hadn't broken his arm. He's not the best in the league. But he is one of the best. He's happy because he's doing something he likes to do. And he's smart. He may not have the fastest fast ball in the big leagues. But they say he's the smartest pitcher in the game.

And there's one more thing. Art's biggest fan is his wife, Patty.

[1]

1

A	B	C
ir	girl	first
ur	fern	turn
er	hurt	thirst
	jerk	her

2

tch

A	B
match	itch
pitcher	catcher
catch	latch

3

flash   chin   also   right   reached   wallet

4

escaped   president   watch   pay   driver

pockets   private   fare   moment   officer

blinked   duds   instant   twenty   hotel

matter   hundred   bride   taking   talking

security   glared   guy   faking   throw

couldn't   once   wig   friend   without   somewhere

5

A Ride to the Docks

The con man and the president had escaped from the hotel. They were in a cab. The con man had gotten rid of his wig and his bridal dress. He was thinking, "The president is very odd. I must leave and hide somewhere."

The president said to the cab driver, "Take us to the docks. We are going to take a trip on a ship because we want to leave this town."

So the cab went to the docks. Then the driver said, "That will be six dollars."

The <u>president</u> turned to the con man. "Private," he said, "pay the driver."

[1]

The con man said, "I don't have any cash. But you have two hundred dollars."

The president said, "Yes, yes. So I do."

Then he reached into his pockets. "I can't seem to find my cash," he said after a moment. The president was faking. He said, "Stay here. I'll be back in a flash with the cash."

The president left the cab and walked up to a woman who looked very rich. The president said, "Where is your pass?"

The woman looked at the president and blinked. "What pass? I don't know what you're talking about."

The president said, "I'm a security officer. You can't be in this part of the docks unless you have a pass. Show me your pass, or I'll have to lock you up."

[2]

"But I don't have a pass," the woman said. "Nobody told me about a pass."

"You had better come along with me, then," the president said, and he grabbed the woman by the arm. He began to lead the woman to the cab.

The woman said, "Wait a moment, officer. Can't I pay you for a pass? If I were to give you some money, couldn't you take care of the matter for me?"

The president asked, "Are you trying to bribe a security officer?"

"No, no," the woman said. "I would never think of doing that. I just had the idea that you might be able to get a pass for me."

[1]

The president rubbed his chin. Then he said, "All right. Give me twenty dollars, and I'll give you a pass. But you must remember that the pass is just good for today. If I ever see you in this spot again without a pass, I'll throw you in jail."

The woman said, "I'll never be here without a pass. I was here to meet a friend who was—"

"Just give me the twenty bucks," the president said.

"Yes, sir," the woman said. She got her wallet and handed the president twenty dollars.

[1]

The president stuck the money in his pocket. Then he took out a pen. "Give me your hand," he said to the woman.

The woman held out her hand, and the president made a big X on the back of the woman's hand. "There," the president said. "Just show that X to any cop who tries to stop you."

"Oh, thank you very much," the woman said.

The president went back to the cab. He asked the driver, "How much was the fare?"

"Six dollars," the cab driver said.

"Here you are, driver," the president said. He handed the cab driver ten dollars. Then he said, "Keep it all."

"Thank you," the driver said.

"That's quite all right," the president said. He smiled.

[2]

Then the president turned to the con man and said, "Private, do you plan to sit in that cab all day? There is no spot in my army for those who sit around."

The con man started to say, "But I was just waiting—"

"Hush up," the president said. "Get out of that cab this instant."

The con man got out of the cab. He was thinking to himself, "I must find a way to get away from this guy."

The president said, "Before we leave on our trip, we must get some fine duds. Who would think of going on a trip without fine duds?"

[1]

1

A	B	C
ir	firm	thirst
ur	surf	serve
er	her	fir
	fur	clerk

2

proudly   batch   our   salt
stormed   pitcher   foolish

3

A	B
up	upset
steam	steamship
over	oversight

4

assistant   door   foolish   Japan   papers
Henry   shocked   strokes
bridal   Robert   expected   shop   dashed
Fredrick   mistake   quickly   Reeves
smiled   bribe   stared   doesn't   lies

5

Sir Robert Fredrick

The president and the con man were at the docks. The president had two hundred and ten dollars. He had gotten two hundred dollars from the hotel by telling the clerk in the hotel that there were bugs in the bridal rooms. When he and the con man went to the docks, the president had gotten twenty dollars from a rich woman. He had given ten dollars to the cab driver.

Now the president and the con man were walking along the docks. The con man asked, "Where are we going?"

The president said, "Will you stop asking foolish questions! We're going on a trip. I need a good rest at sea."

[2]

"But . . . ," the con man started to say.

"Private, if you ever want to become anything but a private, you must remember to take orders. Just do what I tell you to do."

The president and the con man went up to a shop. Over the door of the shop were these words: JAPAN STEAMSHIP LINES.

The president stormed into the shop. He dashed up to the woman at the desk and said, "Just what kind of a line are you running? They tell me that my bags are not here yet. And your man picked them up yesterday."

[1]

The woman behind the desk said, "There must be some mistake. If we picked up your bags, they're here."

"There is a mistake, all right," the president said. "And you made it. How do you expect my assistant and me to go on this trip without our bags? How do you expect us to do our work in Japan if we don't have our papers?"

"I will look into the matter right now," the woman said.

"Before you do," the president said, "let me check on another thing. Where is your list of those who are going on this trip?" The woman handed a list to the president.

[1]

The president looked at the list, and then he said, "Just as I expected. My name is on the list, but my assistant's name is not on the list. I called you three days back and told you that my assistant was going, but you can look for yourself. His name is **not** on this list."

"What is your assistant's name?" the woman asked.

"Reeves. Henry Reeves," the president said.

The woman looked at the list. Then she smiled and said, "You must have looked at the list too quickly. His name is here." The woman held up the list and showed the president.

[1]

The president looked shocked. He stared at the list of names. Then he said, "I am sorry for making such a fuss. I was so upset about our bags that I must have looked right past the name on the list."

The president was telling lies left and right. He had seen the name "Henry Reeves" on the list. In fact, he had looked at the name before he said that his assistant's name was Henry Reeves. The president had just picked a name from the list and had given it to the con man.

[1]

The woman behind the desk stared at the president and asked, "And what is your name?"

The president blinked. "Sir Robert Fredrick," he said proudly.

The woman looked at the list. Then she said, "We have a Robert Fredrick listed here, but the list doesn't show that you are a 'sir.' "

The president stared at the woman behind the desk. "Well, my good woman," the president said, "I think that you can fix that oversight with three strokes of your pen."

"Yes, sir," the woman said. She took her pen and made three strokes: "s-i-r."

The president smiled. "Now if we can find our bags, we will be set for the trip to Japan."

"We will find them," the woman said.

[2]

1

A	B
were	hurt
blur	person
stern	firm
churn	jerk
bird	turn

2

catch   department   loaded   whispered

report   shipping   couldn't   right

waiting   steam   board   our   leave

3

identification   super   office   belonged

fuss   scare   jacket   sorry   fellow

talking   pretend   task

locate   split   assistant

4

A Cartload of Bags

The president and the con man were in the office of the Japan Steamship Lines. The president was telling lies so fast that the con man couldn't keep up with him. The president had looked at the names of those who were going on a ship to Japan. He had picked two names. Then he had told the woman behind the desk that one of the names belonged to the president. Now the woman behind the desk was saying that she would help the president find his bags.

The woman said, "I will make a call to our shipping department and see if we can locate your bags."

As the woman called the shipping department, the president turned to the con man and whispered, "I don't want to tell them that I am a president. That would scare them. So I'll just pretend that I'm another person."

The steamship woman said, "I'm happy to report that all of your bags are safe in our shipping department."

The president turned to the con man and said, "You fool. You told me that our bags were not in the shipping department. You must try to take more care when I give you a task to do."

[1]

The con man didn't say a thing. He just looked at the president. The con man said to himself, "If I am a con man, the president is a super con man."

[2]

The president turned to the woman who worked for the steamship line and told her that he was sorry about making a fuss over the missing bags. He said, "We will go to your shipping department right now and pick up our bags."

The woman said, "Just go up the ramp at the other end of the dock. The ramp leads to the shipping department."

The con man wanted to leave. He said to himself, "I must split. I can't stand this president any longer. I never know what he'll do next."

But the con man didn't leave. He stayed with the president. He walked up the ramp.

[1]

A man in a red jacket was standing at the end of the ramp. The president said, "My name is Sir Robert Fredrick. I have come to pick up my bags."

"Yes, sir," the man said. He waved to another man who was sitting in the middle of the shipping department. That man stood up and came running to the man in the red jacket. "Get Sir Robert's bags," the man in the red jacket said.

The other man dashed off. Soon he came back with a cart loaded with bags. The president nodded. "Yes," he said. "It seems as if they are all here. Take them on board, my good man."

[1]

So the man with the cart took them on board. The president said to the con man, "Follow that fellow. I must go get some more money. We can't have much of a trip if we have only two hundred and ten dollars."

The con man walked behind the man with the cart, and all the time the con man walked, he kept saying to himself, "Now is the time to leave. There is no telling how long that guy can go on before somebody nabs him."

[1]

But just as the con man was ready to split, somebody came up behind him and said, "Just one moment. Those are my bags. Where are you going with them?"

The con man turned around. A tall man was staring at him. The con man stared at the tall man. Then the con man started to say something. But he didn't know what to say. He just said, "Well, I, uh, you see. . . . Well, you know, I, uh. . . ."

The tall man said, "I am waiting for somebody to tell me what you plan to do with my bags."

The con man said, "Well, it's like this, you see. I—that is, we—I mean you. . . ."

The tall man looked very mad.

. [2]

1

found   irk   reached   turned   why
wouldn't   Herb   parked   hush
loan   were   first   clever   match

2

truth   impostor   actor   along   none
flowing   stammering   wonderful
identification   officer   stuttering
demand   wallet   whistle   blast
partner   hollow   hollered   victim
crook   suddenly   buddy   opened

3 # President Washington Tells the Truth

A tall man had found out that the con man was trying to steal his bags. The con man was trying to think of something to say, but the words were not flowing from his mouth. He was stammering and stuttering and saying, "You know—I mean, you see. . . ." The tall man was getting very mad.

Then suddenly the president came back. He had a cop with him. He said, "There he is, officer. That tall man is the impostor. Go ask him his name, and you'll see."

The cop went up to the tall man. "All right, buddy," he said. "What's your name?"

"Fredrick. Robert Fredrick," the tall man said. "And this man seems to be stealing my bags."

[1]

The cop asked, "Do you have identification to show who you are?"

"Yes," the tall man said. He reached in his pocket and grabbed his wallet. As he opened it, the president said, "Just as I told you, officer. That man stole my wallet, and now he's trying to steal our bags."

The cop turned to the tall man. "All right, buddy," he said. "Hand over the wallet."

"I will not!" the man shouted. "That is my wallet. Do you hear me? My wallet! I don't know what's going on here, but I demand—"

"All right, buddy," the cop said. "Come along and pipe down, or I'll have to call the bus that takes you to the rest home."

[2]

"But I haven't done anything," the tall man said. "These men are the crooks."

The cop grabbed the wallet. Then he said, "One more peep out of you, buddy, and I'm calling the bus for the rest home."

"All right," the man said. "I can see that you are part of the plot. You work together to con rich men at the docks."

"That did it," the cop said. He took a whistle from his pocket and gave a loud blast. Soon a bus came up the ramp and parked on the dock.

[1]

Three big cops came out and ran up to the president and the other men. The tall man said, "Please hear what I have to say. I am a victim of a plot to con me. These men have taken my bags and my wallet. Now they are trying to lock me up in a rest home. How can they get away with such a crime? Can't you stop them? Please stop them. Please."

"He is a very good actor," the president said. "If the cops in our wonderful town were not so smart, he would fool them. We are very lucky to have cops who are not fooled by such clever crooks as this tall man."

[2]

"That's right," the first cop said. "This guy can't fool us."

Two cops grabbed the tall man. They started to lead him to the bus. The man began to yell, "Where are you taking me? What are you going to do with me?"

One cop said, "We're taking you to the Happy Hollow Rest Home."

The president said, "One moment, officer. Where did you say you were going?"

"Happy Hollow," the cop said.

The president said, "In that case, I have something to tell you. This man is the real Robert Fredrick. These are his bags, and that wallet is his wallet."

[1]

The con man said, "What are you saying?"

The president hollered, "Hush up, private. Can't you see that I'm talking with this officer?" Then the president went on, "This tall man is the victim of a plot. My partner is really a crook. He is a con man—and not a very good one."

The cop said, "Do you mean that you guys are the crooks, and this tall guy is telling the truth?"

"I wouldn't say that we are crooks. My partner is a crook, but I am a president. And who would ever think that a president could be a crook?"

[1]

1

A	B
home	homesick
every	everything
under	understand

2

thigh perk cheat shout

firm delight curled started

different crouch lurk chain

3

both soldier fares truth

buddy fooled fellow jacket

zoomed sudden trying

stared spent smiling escape sorry

common taking wants impostor

4

Why Did He Tell the Truth?

When the cops said that they were taking the tall man to the Happy Hollow Rest Home, the president began to tell them the truth about everything.

The president was saying, "Yes, the tall man is telling the truth. We were trying to con him out of his bags and his wallet. We have also conned the woman at the steamship line out of two fares to Japan. We conned a rich woman out of twenty dollars, and we conned a hotel out of two hundred dollars and a meal for two. There is <u>more</u> if you want to hear about it."

[1]

The cops let go of the tall man. They stared at the president. The president said, "You must understand that we had to do those things. We are not common crooks. As president, I had to get to Japan. But now things are different."

The cops looked at each other. Then they looked at the con man and the president. One cop asked, "What should we do with these guys?"

The tall man said, "You may start by giving me my wallet. I don't wish to be late for my trip to Japan."

[1]

The cop gave the tall man his wallet. The cop said, "Sorry, buddy. We didn't know that those other guys were con men. They had us fooled."

"That isn't saying very much," the tall man said. He took his wallet and left. The fellow with the red jacket followed with the cartload of bags.

One cop said, "I think we should take both of these guys to the rest home. I think they both are not well."

The president said, "I don't like that kind of talk. If you wish to take us to Happy Hollow, you may do so. But take a little care about how you talk to President Washington."

[2]

"Come on," one cop said. "Get in the bus, and let's go to Happy Hollow."

So the president and the con man got in the bus. And the bus took off down the ramp. As it zoomed down the road, the con man asked, "Why did you do that? All of a sudden you told them everything. We both could have been on that ship to Japan. What made you tell the truth?"

"Private," the president said, "don't talk in that tone."

[1]

The con man said, "Okay. But will you please tell me what got into you? Why did you tell them that we were con men?"

"You are the con man," the president said. "And I've been trying to make you into a soldier. Don't call me a con man."

"All right," the con man said. "Why did you tell them that you were a president and that I was a con man?"

The president didn't say anything. He just curled his lip and stared at the con man.

"Come on," the con man said. "Why did you tell them everything?"

[1]

The president smiled. He said, "It all happened when that one cop said the name Happy Hollow Rest Home."

"What did that name have to do with it?" the con man asked.

"I have spent three years at Happy Hollow," the president said. He was still smiling. "Those were the best three years of my life. When the cop said, 'Happy Hollow,' I became homesick." The president had a tear in his eye.

The con man had two tears in his eyes. But his tears were not tears of delight. He was thinking that he would have to start all over. He would have to plan some way to get out of the rest home. He said to himself, "And the next time I escape, I won't be conned into going with a guy like the president."

[2]

1

Hurn mouth ferns sharp air
also breathing hurled fir
would crouched faith Surt
poach jerk ouch slashed

2

forward beware except dead
both stiff two knowing clover
against snapped sniffed wolves
safe fixed battled happened
sister smelled peered neck

3

Hurn, the Wolf

Hurn was sleeping when it happened. Hurn didn't hear the big cat sneak into the cave that Hurn called his home. Suddenly Hurn was awake. Something told him, "Beware!" His eyes turned to the darkness near the mouth of the cave. Hurn felt the fur on the back of his neck stand up. His nose, like noses of all wolves, was very keen. It made him very happy when it smelled something good. But now it smelled something that made him afraid.

Hurn was five months old. He had never seen a big cat. He had seen clover and ferns and grass. He had even eaten rabbits.

[1]

Hurn's mother had come back with them after she had been hunting. She had always come back. And Hurn had always been glad to see her. But now she was not in the cave.

Hurn's sister, Surt, was the only happy smell that reached Hurn's nose.

Surt was awake. She was leaning against Hurn, and Hurn could feel how hard Surt was shaking.

"Oooooowww," howled Surt. At the sound of the howl, Hurn jerked. Then he turned his nose back toward the mouth of the cave. He made his ears stand up as high as they would go. Adult wolves have ears that stand up all the way. But puppy wolves, like Hurn, have ears that stand up part way. Then they flop forward.

[2]

Suddenly Hurn's ears grabbed something from the air. They grabbed the sound of a padded paw taking a slow step across the floor of the cave. Then another padded paw came down slowly on the cave floor.

"Run, run," something told Hurn. But there was nowhere to run. Hurn peered at the mouth of the cave. He crouched down as low as he could get, and looked. Then he saw the outline of the big cat. The cat was bigger than Hurn's mother. It was only about two meters from Hurn and it was walking slowly toward Hurn and his sister.

[1]

Hurn tried to back away. But he felt the hard rock of the cave against his back. He could go back no more. Surt was curled next to Hurn.

Without knowing why he did it, Hurn showed his teeth and began to growl. He snapped at the air as if to scare the cat away. The cat stopped for an instant, but then it started to come toward the puppies again.

Suddenly something dashed into the cave. It growled and it slashed at the cat. It was Hurn's mother. She had come back to her puppies. She hurled herself at the cat. The cat spun across and met with sharp claws. Bits of fur floated in the air as the mother wolf battled the cat. Then the cat ran from the cave.

[2]

The mother wolf walked very slowly to Hurn and Surt. She sniffed them. She licked Hurn on the ear. Then she curled up next to her pups. Hurn got as close to her as he could get. She felt good.

Hurn couldn't see that she had been badly hurt in the fight with the cat. He couldn't see that her eyes were fixed and that she was breathing slower and slower.

Hurn went to sleep, feeling very safe. When he woke in the morning, he could feel that something was wrong. His mother was cold, and she was stiff.

His mother was dead and Hurn was all alone, except for his little sister, Surt.

[2]

1 fir churning mountain thirsty
catch sheath reach whirl bald

2 toward paw rabbits
prodded cried howled died scared

3 cool instant dead kilometer
stream lonely litter sniff
shivering drank bank quickly
scanning fire didn't don't
smelled hungry won't wheeze
rolling rounded cooking chase

The Hunter's Camp

Hurn's mother had been in a fight with a big cat. She scared the cat from the cave, but the cat had won the fight. Hurn's mother died that night.

At first, Hurn cried and howled. He prodded his mother with his nose. He gave her a little bite on her ear. But she lay still. So Hurn cried and howled.

Surt cried, too. For most of the day, they stayed by their mother. They didn't go out to run after butterflies. They didn't chase rabbits. They didn't even want to go to the stream for a drink and a cool swim. They sat near their mother and waited for her to get up. But she didn't get up.

[2]

When the afternoon sun was getting near the tops of the fir trees, Surt walked over to Hurn and bit him on the tail. In an instant, Hurn turned around and bit his sister on the throat. It was a play bite, but it was the kind of bite that big wolves give when they are hunting.

Soon Surt and her brother were rolling and churning on the ground. For a moment, Hurn was happy, but the moment passed quickly. As suddenly as the pups had started playing, they stopped and sat. They sat and looked at their mother.

[1]

Later, when the sun could no longer be seen over the tops of the fir trees, Surt ran from the cave. She ran down the slope that led to the stream. With Surt gone, Hurn began to feel very lonely. So he followed his little sister.

Although Surt had been born before Hurn, Surt was smaller than Hurn. There had been another wolf born in the same litter as Hurn and Surt, but she had died. Hurn's mother had been less than two years old when Hurn and Surt were born. They were the only two pups she ever raised.

[1]

Surt was the first one to reach the stream. She jumped in the water. Then she began to bite the water. "Rrrr," she said as she bit.

Hurn ran after his sister. Again the pups began to play and fight in the water.

"Barooo."

The pups stopped playing and held their ears as high as they would go. The sound that reached them was from a gun.

Less than a kilometer away was the camp of three hunters. Surt and Hurn didn't know it then, but one of those hunters had just shot a cat as it tried to attack. It was the big cat that had killed their mother.

[1]

The pups stood in the cold water, shivering and scanning the air with their noses. Slowly the pups walked from the water. But they did not go back to the cave. Something told them that the cave was no longer safe. Something said to Hurn, "Stay away from the cave."

So Hurn and Surt began to follow the bank of the stream. Hurn led the way. Surt followed. From time to time she tried to play with her brother, but Hurn wouldn't play.

[1]

Hurn didn't feel like a puppy right now. He didn't want to sniff things for the fun of sniffing. He didn't want to hear things just to hear them. He wanted to find something, but he didn't know what. He did know that he was hungry.

Hurn told himself that he was thirsty. So he drank from the stream. But the water didn't help. He wanted something to eat.

The pups didn't know it, but they were very close to the hunters' camp. In fact, they would be able to see the camp when they rounded the next bend in the stream.

[1]

Hurn sniffed the air. He smelled smoke. The smell told him to go the other way. "Run from that smell," something told him.

But then another smell came to Hurn's nose. It was the smell of meat cooking on an open fire. "Eat that," something told Hurn. He felt his mouth begin to water. He stood there trying to figure out what he should do. Should he run from the smell of the smoke, or should he run toward the smell of the cooking meat?

Surt helped Hurn to make up his mind. Surt began running toward the smell of the meat. Hurn followed.

[1]

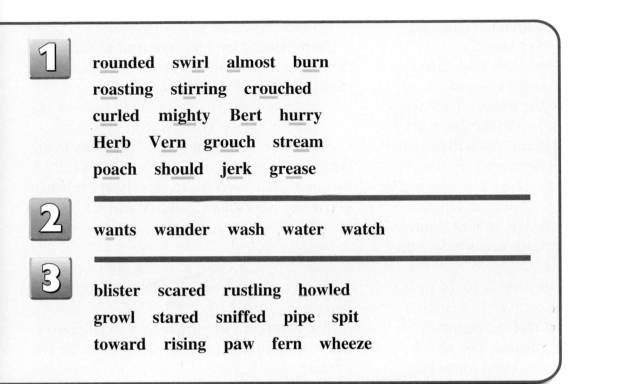

1
rounded swirl almost burn
roasting stirring crouched
curled mighty Bert hurry
Herb Vern grouch stream
poach should jerk grease

2
wants wander wash water watch

3
blister scared rustling howled
growl stared sniffed pipe spit
toward rising paw fern wheeze

4

Surt Goes for the Meat

Surt was running toward the hunters' camp. Hurn was following. As Hurn rounded a bend in the stream, he could see a swirl of smoke rising from the campfire. A man was bent over the fire, stirring a pot of beans. Next to the beans was a deer leg roasting on a spit. Another hunter was turning the spit. The men were talking.

"Did you see the marks on that cat?" one man said. "It looked like that cat was in a whale of a fight."

"That cat was in such bad shape that it dropped before you shot it," another hunter said. He and a third man began to laugh.

The first man said, "Come on, you guys. That was a good shot."

[2]

Hurn hid behind a fern. His mouth was watering. He was staring at the deer leg on the spit. He wanted to dash over to the spit and grab it and take a big bite from it. But he looked and waited.

"Hey, Herb," one of the men yelled. "How long before those beans are ready? I'm getting mighty hungry."

"Look, Vern, if you want to fix the beans, you can take over any time you want. But if you want me to fix them, you'll have to wait."

"What a grouch!" the third man said.

[1]

Suddenly the man turning the spit jumped up. "Ow," he yelled.

The man who had been stirring the beans said, "What's wrong, Bert?"

"Some grease popped out and landed on my arm. Boy, does that ever burn!"

"Soak it in cold water," Vern said. "Do it right away, and you won't get a blister."

Vern and Bert ran to the stream. They ran past Hurn and his sister. Hurn bent down close to the ground. He laid his ears back flat against his neck. He was very scared.

[1]

"That water feels good," Bert said. "You should go back and stir those beans before they burn. That fire is really hot."

"Let me see your arm. Turn it so the light shines on it."

Suddenly there was a rustling sound in the ferns next to Hurn. Hurn turned. The sound came from Surt. She was running toward the spit. She was running as fast as her legs would take her. She reached the spit before any of the men saw her, and she might have gotten away with a big chunk of deer meat—except for one thing. She stepped in the fire. She had never seen fire before. She had been in such a hurry to get the meat that she didn't take as much care as she should have.

[2]

"Oooowww," Surt howled.

"What was that . . . ? Hey, look at that dog!"

"That's no dog. That's a wolf! And it's after our dinner. Vern, shoot it."

"Shoot it," the other man yelled.

Vern walked over to Surt. Surt crouched down. She curled up her lip and showed her teeth, but she did not growl.

"Did you burn yourself?" Vern said softly.

"Shoot it, Vern. That's a wolf. Shoot it."

Vern didn't say anything to the other men. He bent down and cut a chunk of meat from the roast. He tossed it to Surt. The meat landed in front of Surt's nose, but Surt did not look at the meat. She stared at Vern.

[1]

Hurn crouched behind a fern and stared at Surt.

Vern walked away from Surt. "Get your gun and shoot it," the men yelled from the stream.

Finally Vern turned to them and said, "Will you guys shut up? That is just a little puppy. And it's hungry. So just pipe down."

Surt sniffed the meat two times. Then, with a jerk, she took it in her mouth. She gulped it down. Like all wolves, Surt ate fast. A wolf never knows when it will eat again. The meat will stay with it longer if the meat is not broken into many little bits.

[1]

1 jerked swirled sparks chunk
watched crouched stirring snail
croaking breathed Vern burned

2 wagged gulp hoot sometimes
owl fiddle howling water
limping paw followed Bert
friends orange poke want

3

Surt and Vern

Hurn was watching from behind a fern. He saw the man called Vern give a chunk of meat to Surt. He saw Surt eat the meat. Hurn crouched down low as the other men came back from the stream. When they reached the campfire, Surt ran away on three legs. She held one leg high. That was the leg that had been burned when Surt stepped in the fire.

"Grab it, Vern," one of the men yelled.

Vern said, "Let it go. Do you have to kill everything you see?"

Surt did not run back toward Hurn. She began running up the hill on the far side of the camp.

[1]

When Surt was about twenty-five meters from the men, she stopped and looked back. Then she sat down and began to lick her sore paw.

Vern cut another chunk of meat from the roast and walked over to Surt. Slowly Vern bent down and held out the meat. "Are you still hungry?" Vern asked.

At first, Surt laid her ears back and curled up her lip. But then her ears began to stand up again. Vern was very still. And so was Surt. Surt sniffed the meat. Then she slowly took it in her mouth. "Gulp." She ate it.

Vern began to stand up, and when he did, Surt jerked back. "It's all right," Vern said, and Surt wagged her tail.

[1]

"What are you doing?" one of the men yelled. "Don't make friends with that wolf. Wolves are killers."

"So are hunters," Vern said.

Vern walked back to the campfire. The night sky was clear, and it was filled with stars and a bright moon. The smoke from the fire swirled up like a white band into the night sky. And the orange sparks jumped from the fire and followed the swirling band of smoke. A group of frogs was croaking in the stream. From the forest came the sounds of a hoot owl, "Hoo, hoo."

[1]

One of the men was stirring the beans. Another was sitting near the spit. Vern sat on the other side of the fire. And Hurn was trying to hear everything and see everything. But he didn't move. The only things that moved were his sides as he breathed.

"The beans are done," one man said. "In fact, they're burned on the bottom."

"Let's eat," another man said.

The men took tin plates and heaped beans on them. Then the men cut big slabs of deer meat and piled them on their plates. Then they ate. Hurn's mouth began to water as he watched them, but he didn't move.

[1]

The men went back for more beans and more meat, and Hurn's mouth watered more.

"I've had all I can eat," one man said.

"Me, too," said another man. "And we still have almost all of the roast left."

One of the men went to the tent and came back with a fiddle. He began to play.

Hurn turned his ears so that they could catch the funny sounds.

Sometimes they felt good. Sometimes they hurt. And there were times when they made Hurn want to start howling. But he didn't howl.

When the man began to play the fiddle, Vern lay down on his back and closed his eyes. The other man sat in front of the fire and lit his pipe. That man said, "That sounds really fine, Bert."

[2]

Then something funny happened. As the man played the fiddle, Surt began to walk slowly down the hill toward the men. She was still limping, but she walked on all of her paws. She walked over to Vern and sat down next to him. The men did not see her do this.

Surt sniffed the air. She was smelling the meat. She wanted some more meat, but she wanted something else, too. She missed her mother. She wanted a friend. So she leaned over and gave Vern a little poke with her nose.

Vern opened his eyes and smiled. "What have we here?" he asked. Slowly he moved his hand toward Surt. Surt smelled the hand. Then Surt let Vern pat her on her neck. Surt wagged her tail again.

[2]

1

A	B
it	itself
bull	bullfrog
butter	butterflies

2

purple croak whisper lurking

morning soaked dream whack

thirty tail groan fern firm chill

3

patting washing charge snapped

chasing problems wagged tugging

sneaked walking insects snooze

hopped forward tried wandered

done friends breeze doesn't tame

Hurn Is Alone

Surt had tried to make friends with Vern. The other men hadn't seen Surt walk down the hill and come over to Vern. Now Vern was patting Surt, and Surt's tail was wagging.

One of the other men turned around. "Hey, what's going on?" he snapped. "You can't make friends with that wolf. Get it out of here."

Vern said, "Look, Bert, did you ever ask yourself what a wolf this old is doing out at night all by itself? Wolves this old are with their mothers—when they have mothers. I'll bet this little wolf doesn't have a <u>mother</u>."

"So what?" Bert said. "Wolves are no good. They kill other animals."

Vern said, "When wolves aren't around, things get out of whack. Too many of the other animals live. Then we have real problems."

Bert said, "Well, keep that thing away from me. I hate wolves."

At that moment, something told Hurn to leave. Something told him that Surt was no longer his sister. Hurn was right, but he didn't know it then. Vern would keep Surt, and Surt would become as tame as most dogs. She would live with Vern, and she would love Vern almost as much as she had loved her mother. And Vern would love her.

[1]

[1]

At that moment, Hurn did not know all of these things. But he felt something tugging at him, telling him to leave. And so he left.

As he did, he felt very sad and very hungry. He sneaked back along the stream, back around the bend. Now he could no longer see the light of the campfire. He could still hear the men talking, but he couldn't hear what they said.

Hurn went to the bank of the stream and began to drink. The water was cold, and it gave him a chill. He could feel the cool night breeze cut into his fur.

[1]

Hurn wanted to curl up and sleep. He wanted to dream about eating or running or chasing butterflies. But when he was done with his drink, he began walking upstream along the bank of the stream.

He felt like going back to the cave, but he didn't remember how to get to the cave. And he remembered that the cave was not his home any more. He had to find a new cave. He had to find a friend. So he walked and walked.

[1]

The coldest part of the night comes just before the sun comes up. The air is often still then, and some fog hangs at the top of the fir trees. The morning birds begin to sing while the frogs and some of the night insects get ready for a snooze. And then the sky to the east begins to turn light purple.

When the sky began to turn light purple that morning, Hurn was still walking along the bank of the stream. He had walked over five kilometers from the camp, and he was very tired.

He had stopped only a few times after he left the camp. Once he had tried to catch a bull frog that was sitting on a log. Hurn jumped at the frog, but the frog gave out with a big croak and hopped from the log just before Hurn's teeth reached the log. Hurn fell in the water and got his fur soaked.

[2]

Now things seemed so bad that Hurn sat down and began to howl. He didn't know why he was howling. It just seemed that howling would help. "Ooooowww," he howled.

Hurn must have howled thirty times when suddenly he knew that something was staring at him. He stopped and sniffed the air. He leaned forward and held his nose close to the ground to catch any smell that was down there. Then he held his nose as high as he could make it go.

He smelled nothing. But there was something staring at him. Hurn's ears told him that. Something was lurking in the dark, staring at the little wolf pup.

[2]

1

A	B	C	D	E
set	rod	pan	bed	cam
seat	rode	pane	bead	came

2

birth   crouched   whined   throat   burp
treated   attached   breathed   whirl

3

hollow   cliff   growl   shoot
upwind   blowing   snuggled   cocked
scanning   watching   sneaked   mixed
stiffly   paw   puffs   person   goal
realized   asleep   tugged   nipped
grown   yawned   lasted   who   stood

4

The Tan Wolf

Hurn had been walking along the stream all night. Then he had stopped and begun to howl. He stopped howling when he felt that something was watching.

And there *was* something that was watching him. It was a big tan wolf. She was less than three meters from Hurn. She had come down to the stream when Hurn first began to howl. She had left her pup asleep in a hollow just below a cliff. And she had sneaked down.

Now she was standing behind a fir tree, looking at Hurn. She was upwind from him. Like all good hunters, she moved so that the breeze was blowing toward her. The breeze was blowing from Hurn toward the tan wolf. That way, Hurn couldn't smell her.

[1]

That tan wolf didn't know what to make of Hurn. She knew that he wasn't a grown wolf. Her nose told her that. But she also knew that he wasn't one of her pups. She missed her pups. She had given birth to six pups. That was three months back. All of the pups but one had died. She missed them, but she knew that Hurn was not hers. And yet—she wanted another pup.

She slowly moved from behind the fir tree. Now Hurn saw her. At first he just stood there with his ears cocked and his eyes staring at her and his nose scanning the air. But then he realized that she was a hunter. He crouched and began to growl. "Grrrrr," he growled.

[1]

She kept on moving toward him. Hurn showed his teeth. He curled his lip. He growled louder. But she kept coming.

Then Hurn became very mixed up. He could smell that she was a friend—a wolf. So he wagged his tail and turned over on his back. But he was still scared.

The tan wolf bent over and smelled him. The fur on the back of her neck stood up. If he had moved quickly right then, she might have killed him. But he didn't move. He whined a little and tried to lick her.

[1]

The tan wolf jerked back stiffly. Then she bent forward once more. She sniffed the pup. Again he licked her and began to wag his tail. She sniffed him five or six times. Then she turned and began to walk away.

When the tan wolf began to leave, Hurn jumped up and ran after her. He grabbed her back leg and bit her. He was playing and trying to show her that he liked her. But she did not know how to act. At first her fur stood up, and she let out a growl from deep in her throat. Then she bent down and sniffed the pup again. He hit her nose with his paw, and then he bit at her ear. She stood very still. He tugged at her ear.

[2]

Suddenly the tan wolf nipped him. That nip hurt, and Hurn rolled over on his back. When he did that, he showed her that he would do what she wanted him to do. Now she knew that he would follow her to her den. She wanted him to follow her.

Hurn was very lucky. He was not a good hunter yet. He could fight pretty well, but he wouldn't have lasted in the forest. If he had been a little older, this mother wolf wouldn't have wanted him in her den. She would have treated him as a grown wolf and attacked him. Maybe she would have killed him.

[1]

So Hurn followed the tan wolf back to her den. There he met her pup. He was sleeping, curled up in a little ball. Hurn sniffed him, and the tan wolf stared at Hurn. When she felt that Hurn would not harm her pup, she yawned. Then she turned around three times and lay down with her nose toward the opening of the den.

Hurn snuggled up next to her. They looked like two balls of fur. The birds were making sounds. The sky was light purple over the tall fir trees. The morning air was cold, and little puffs of steam came from Hurn's nose as he breathed. And Hurn was so, so tired. He blinked two times. Then his eyes closed, and he was asleep.

[2]

1

A	B	C	D	E
bite	meat	pine	feed	note
bit	met	pin	fed	not

2

spark   bold   toad   eating

wail   hoot   bright   nor

3

woke   blinked   clearing   slope

moment   grown   messed   except

ready   snapped   rolled   nipped

eye   scar   past   idea   yelped

different   growl   stared   pack

4

Hurn Meets the Wolf Pack

Hurn slept like a log that night. He woke up once when the tan wolf left the den, but he went back to sleep in a moment. When he woke up the next time, the sun was high in the sky. The air was almost hot, and things looked so bright outside the den that Hurn blinked. The tan wolf was not around, nor was her pup.

Hurn walked from the den, and then he stopped. There was a big, black wolf standing on the slope. That wolf was looking at Hurn. Another wolf, a brown one, was also looking at Hurn. Far on the other side of the clearing were the tan wolf and her pup.

[1]

Something told Hurn to stay away from the other wolves, so he began to walk toward the tan wolf. Then he began to run.

Hurn didn't know that the tan wolf was part of a wolf pack. There were 8 wolves in the pack. The tan wolf had kept to herself for a time after she had her pups. Any grown wolf who came near her den was asking for a good fight. The tan wolf could beat up any wolf in the pack except the black wolf. No wolf messed with him.

[1]

Now that the tan wolf's pup was older, she had begun to mix with the other wolves again. She still kept to herself at night, but in the daytime she went out with her pup. Sometimes she hunted with the pack.

Hurn didn't know all this. He just knew that he didn't feel safe with those other wolves. So he ran as fast as he could toward the tan wolf. But he didn't make it. The brown wolf ran in front of him and cut him off.

[1]

Hurn stopped and laid his ears back. The brown wolf was a little more than a year old. He was not yet a good hunter. He wasn't a grown wolf yet, but he liked to think that he was. He was as big as a grown wolf, and he was always ready to show the others how good he was.

The brown wolf made a quick pass at Hurn. Hurn jumped back. Then the brown wolf nipped Hurn on the back. Hurn turned around. The brown wolf was quick. He jumped over Hurn and bit Hurn on the side. Then he bit Hurn's tail.

[1]

Hurn turned and snapped. This time his teeth bit into the brown wolf's leg. The brown wolf let out a high growl and bit Hurn very hard on the side of the neck. He held onto Hurn with his mouth and began to shake his head from one side to the other.

Hurn started to cry. His neck hurt and that brown wolf wouldn't let go. "Owwwww," he cried.

His cry reached the tan wolf. She left her pup and ran over to Hurn. She didn't growl.

She didn't let the brown wolf know what she was going to do. She ran into him and rolled him over.

[1]

Then she bit the brown wolf just under the eye. He would have a scar from that bite for the rest of his life.

The brown wolf yelped and ran up the slope. Then the tan wolf turned and walked over to Hurn. He was on the ground, crying. She licked his neck. Then she stood up and stared at the other wolves. That was her way of saying, "This little wolf is mine. If you mess with him, you will have to fight me." She even looked the black wolf right in the eyes. She was saying, "That goes for you, too."

[1]

Then the tan wolf began to walk up the slope, past the other wolves. When she was part way up the slope, she stopped and waited for Hurn. He ran up behind her and tried to hide under her. She held her head up and walked on past the other wolves. They stared at her as she passed.

Hurn felt very safe when he was near the tan wolf. And he felt that way for some time. He stayed with her that fall. He stayed near her in the long winter. When she went hunting, he waited with her pup. She always came back, and she always had food. She shared that food with Hurn. Hurn loved her. He felt sad when she left. He never had an idea that someday things would be different.

But then one day, almost a year after he had come to the wolf pack, something happened.

[2]

1

A	**B**
bend	melt
bead	meet

C	**D**
sent	gold
seat	good

2

burn   streaks   smarter
jerked   bright

3

puzzled   jogged   smelled
gazed   showed   stared
rolled   whined   wagged
belly   grow   slope   path
hollow   darker   silver
except   checks   meaner
chasing   grown   wanted
loved   welcome   daytime

4

Things Change for Hurn

Hurn had lived with the tan wolf for nearly a year. She had been like a mother to him. He loved her. That is why he was so puzzled that day when he came back to the den. He had been hunting with some of the other wolves. Hurn was getting to be a fair hunter. He had helped the pack bring down a small deer. He had hunted for rabbits and pack rats. Hurn was feeling more like a grown wolf every day. He jogged up the path to his den, just as he had many times before.

[1]

But when he got near the den, the tan wolf met him. She gazed at him in a funny way. Hurn stopped. Then he began to walk toward her. She crouched down and showed her teeth. "Grrr," she growled.

She was trying to tell Hurn something, but he didn't get what it was. She was trying to say, "I am going to have pups in a day or two. That means that you must leave. No more are you a pup. No more are you welcome in this den."

[1]

She didn't look as if she wanted to play, but Hurn began to think that maybe she wanted to play. So he jumped toward her. She jerked back and growled louder. Hurn didn't know what to do. So he started to go into the den. She growled again and bit him on the back. She rolled him over and bit him again and again. Then she turned and walked away from him.

Hurn whined and stood up. He wagged his tail and got down on his belly. He was trying to show her that he didn't want to fight. She didn't look at him. She stood in front of the den, looking up the hill.

[1]

When Hurn stood up, she turned toward him and growled again. "Go away," she was trying to say. "I don't want to hurt you, but I will if you come near this den."

At first, Hurn stood and whined. Then he turned and walked away. Hurn was hurt, and he didn't know what to do. He didn't know that the tan wolf was helping him grow up. He just knew that he was hurt.

He walked up the slope to a hollow where some of the other wolves stayed. The brown wolf stayed there. So did the big black wolf.

[1]

Hurn didn't know if the wolves would beat him up or let him stay with them. But he didn't know where else he could go. So he walked up to the hollow.

The black wolf was sitting on a log next to the hollow. He stood up when Hurn came near. He walked over to Hurn. Hurn lay down and rolled over on his back. That was his way of saying that he knew that the black wolf was the boss. So the black wolf let him stay.

[1]

To Hurn, the nights didn't seem to be as much fun as they had been when he was with the tan wolf. Even in the daytime, Hurn didn't play so much. He didn't want to have fun. He wanted something, but he didn't know what. He didn't know that he wanted to be a grown wolf.

As Hurn got older, his fur turned darker. At first, it was silver with streaks of black. Now he was all black, except for his cheeks. They were still silver. He looked a lot like the big black wolf, except that the black wolf was a little fatter than he was.

[1]

The black wolf was also a little meaner and a little smarter. Hurn found that out one day.

It happened when the pack was hunting. They were chasing a fox. The fox was very smart. The fox would bite off bits of fur and drop them on the bank of the stream. Then the fox would swim to the other side of the stream. The idea was to get the wolves mixed up.

And the plan almost worked. The wolves came to the bank of the stream. They smelled the bits of fur. The smell was very strong. It was so strong that the wolves could smell nothing else. They ran around and around, but they always came back to the bits of fur.

[2]

1

A	B	C	D	E
spend	bolt	tart	help	loud
speed	bout	tail	heap	lead

2

trail   torn   heaved

mountain   swirled   meters

3

December   swam   stood   rare   poor

quicker   quite   badly   lurched

bleeding   spring   quickly   drifts   tire

twenty   male   skinny   flowing

hungry   flowers   valley   seventy

The Fight

The fox had a trick that almost worked, but the black wolf was not fooled. He did not run around and around like Hurn and the other wolves. He walked to the middle of the stream. He held his nose high and stood there for a long time. He was trying to get a fresh smell from the air. At last he did. He swam to the other side of the stream. He howled to let the other wolves know that he had found the trail.

The wolves had a good meal that night. But there weren't as many good meals as there had been last year.

[1]

The pack was getting too big. Some of the wolves would have to leave. Hurn didn't know it, but he was one of those wolves. The brown wolf, Hurn, and two other wolves would not go back with that pack that night.

When the wolves had eaten the fox, the black wolf walked over and bit the brown wolf. The brown wolf howled but he didn't fight back. Then the black wolf bit Hurn. Hurn did not howl. The fur on Hurn's back stood up, and Hurn began to fight with the black wolf. Hurn wanted to hurt that black wolf, and he didn't know why. He had lived with the black wolf, but something told him to fight. Something told him to win.

[1]

The other wolves backed away as Hurn and the black wolf went at it. When wolves are really fighting, they can move very fast, and they can bite very hard. It is rare when one wolf kills another wolf, but it is not rare when one wolf hurts another wolf quite badly.

Hurn got hurt quite badly. He was quicker than the black wolf, but not as smart. He lurched at the black wolf, and the black wolf crouched down.

[1]

When Hurn went for the black wolf's neck, the black wolf went for Hurn's belly. When Hurn curled up so that the black wolf could not get at his belly, the black wolf went for Hurn's neck. Again and again, the black wolf got the best of Hurn.

Hurn was bleeding. His ear was torn. His belly was cut badly. So was his neck. But he kept lurching at the black wolf. And each time he did, the black wolf got the best of him.

Now Hurn was starting to tire. He didn't spring at the black wolf so quickly. The black wolf didn't have such a hard time rolling Hurn over.

[1]

Then Hurn stopped. He was in pain, but more than that, he was tired. He was so tired that he could hardly hold up his head. His sides heaved in and out as he breathed. He looked at the black wolf as if to say, "Okay. You win." But his look told the black wolf, "You win this time, but I may be back."

Then Hurn and three other wolves stood there and watched the other wolves go back to their dens. Hurn knew that he was not welcome. So Hurn and the other wolves left.

[1]

Hurn became the boss of those wolves. He didn't have to fight any of them. They seemed to know that he was boss. Maybe they knew from the way that he had gone at the black wolf.

Late in the fall, Hurn led the other wolves to high ground, way up the side of a mountain. They would spend the winter up there, and they would not have an easy time. The trees were not tall, and there were not many animals.

The snow came early. It swirled down from the top of the mountain every night. Before the middle of December, the snow had piled up in drifts that were seven meters high.

[1]

The winter was long for that pack of wolves, and the hunting was poor. They spent most of their time sleeping. When they were asleep, they didn't feel so hungry.

By spring, the wolves were so skinny that their long fur couldn't hide their ribs. They were almost too hungry to feel hunger. When they went from one spot to another spot, they walked slowly. They didn't want to burn up their food any faster than they had to.

The snow on the mountain was wet. Little white flowers peeked out of cracks in the rocks. The streams were flowing fast down the side of the mountain. Hurn and the other wolves were on their way to the green valley below.

[2]

1

A	B
foam	belt
form	Bert

C	D
roam	mark
room	mask

2

nearly mood starved

steep mounted

3

bothered friendly pretty
because hundred panting
dashed somehow followed
nape yelp half kilometer
hungry growled two
winner woman wouldn't
brother tired tried

4

The Leader of the Pack

As Hurn and the other wolves slowly walked down the side of the mountain, a big black bear came out of its den. The bear had been sleeping nearly all winter, and it was mean and hungry. The bear stood up and growled at the wolves. They turned and began to walk away.

The bear was not in a friendly mood. "Grrrrr," it growled, and started to chase Hurn and the other wolves.

Down the mountainside they went. The wolves had to run pretty fast because that bear was fast. The wolves ran about half a kilometer. They were panting. The bear was panting, too.

[1]

Suddenly Hurn stopped. The other wolves kept running, but something told Hurn that he would run no more. He would turn around and fight that bear.

Wolves fight bears sometimes, but that is rare. Even when wolves are very hungry, they will not bother bears. Sometimes a big pack of wolves will attack a bear, but wolves must be almost starved before they'll do that. Hurn was hungry, but he wasn't almost starved. And he didn't plan to fight with the help of other wolves. He just didn't want to run from that bear any more.

[1]

So he stopped where the slope of the mountain was not too steep. He crouched down and waited for the bear. The bear stood up and began to come at Hurn on two legs.

Hurn didn't move until the bear was about two meters from him. Then Hurn dashed at the bear's left leg. He dug his teeth into the leg and ran behind the bear before the bear could take a swing at Hurn. Hurn had fur in his mouth.

The bear turned around. Hurn stayed behind and again went for the bear's left leg. The bear dropped down on all its legs now. As soon as it did, Hurn lurched at the bear and sank his teeth into the bear's nose.

[1]

Bears are funny. Sometimes they will fight, and sometimes they will run away. Their noses are very tender, and a good bite on the nose will make them madder or will take the fight from them.

Hurn's bite took the fight from this bear. The bear rubbed its nose on the ground. It looked at Hurn and began to think, "Maybe I don't want to fight this wolf any more." The bear stood up again and growled, just to let Hurn know that it could fight if it wanted to. Then the bear turned around and began to walk up the side of the mountain.

[1]

The other wolves had seen what Hurn did. Somehow they knew that Hurn was a leader wolf like no other wolf. And they were right. Later that year, Hurn went back to the black wolf's pack. He had another fight with the black wolf. This time Hurn was the winner.

The black wolf left the pack, and Hurn became the leader.

For nine years Hurn led the pack. For nine years he led the wolves when they hunted. And at night he walked around sniffing the air and seeing to it that his pack was safe.

[1]

And one night while Hurn was on patrol, the sound of a howling wolf came from the other side of the slope. Hurn followed the sound. When he got near, he could see a wolf pup stuck in a crack between two rocks. The pup had fallen from above and couldn't get out.

Hurn could have walked away from the wolf, but he remembered something about when he was a wolf pup. There was something about that pup in the rocks that made Hurn think way back to Surt, and to the time when Hurn was alone.

[1]

So Hurn didn't walk away from the wolf pup. Hurn got above the wolf pup and grabbed her by the nape of her neck. He gave a hard jerk. The pup let out a yelp, but now the pup was free. The pup wagged her tail and rolled over on her back to show Hurn that he was boss and that she would do what he wanted her to do.

Hurn walked back toward his den, just as the tan wolf had done years ago. And that wolf pup followed, just as Hurn had followed the tan wolf years and years ago.

[2]

1

oi

<u>A</u>   <u>B</u>

oil   point

boil   noise

2

gr<u>ee</u>t   st<u>ar</u>ved   compl<u>ai</u>n   l<u>ou</u>sy   f<u>o</u>lded

3

<u>mustard</u>   <u>instead</u>   lived   wanted

cheese   kitchen   factory   French

settled   fries   experiment   Irma

terms   clothes   evening   smile

lazy   dryer   invent   inventor

watching   boarding   Berta   Carl

basement   o'clock   lab   someday

4

Why Irma Boils

There once was a woman named Irma. Irma ran a boarding house. Seven people lived in her boarding house. They slept in the boarding house, ate in this house, and paid Irma for their rooms and meals. But they did not treat Irma very well.

Carl and Herman were brothers who lived on the second floor of the house. Herman worked in an oil plant. Carl toiled in a meat plant. The two brothers did not get along with each other.

Berta was a loud woman who lived on the first floor. She didn't have a job. She spent most of her time watching <u>TV</u>. Three women lived on the third floor of Irma's boarding house. All worked in a cheese factory. Irma worked in that factory, too.

Every evening, Irma came home very tired. But nobody greeted her at the door with a smile. Herman would usually be standing near the door. He would say, "It's about time you got home. Now go out and get some hamburgers for us to eat. We are starved."

So Irma would go out and get the hamburgers. And when she would come back, Berta wouldn't say, "Irma, it's very good of you to get those hamburgers." Instead she'd say, "It's about time you got back. I'll bet the hamburgers are cold."

[1]

[1]

Then everybody would sit down and eat. And all the time they ate, they would complain to Irma. "This hamburger has mustard on it," Herman would say. "Irma, you know that I can't stand mustard."

Then Herman's brother would say, "Where are the French fries? You know I can't eat hamburgers without French fries."

Irma wouldn't say anything. She would sit there and boil. She would think to herself, "Someday I'll get even with them for every mean thing they do to me."

But Irma was not a fighter. She wanted to be on good terms with everybody. She wanted people to like her.

[1]

After dinner, all the people who lived in Irma's boarding house would get up from the table. "That was a lousy meal," they would say. Then they would go into the living room and watch TV.

As they watched TV, somebody would clean up the mess at the table. That somebody was Irma. Then maybe Irma would sit down in her chair in the kitchen. By now she would be very tired. But just about the time she got settled in her chair, somebody would yell from the living room, "Is somebody going to wash the clothes this evening?"

And who do you think that somebody was?

[1]

That's right. Irma washed the clothes. She wadded up the dirty clothes and dumped them into the washer. She put soap in the tub.

"Irma," Berta called, "don't put the sheets in with those dark clothes."

"Yes, Berta," Irma said.

There were other things that she wanted to do. She would have liked to watch TV. Even more than that, she would have liked to work in her lab. She had a lab down in the basement. She liked to work there because nobody bothered her.

[1]

They all said, "It stinks in that lab. Why don't you throw all of that junk out?" But that is one thing that Irma didn't do for them. She kept her lab. She kept the bottles, the pans, and all of the other things that she needed for her experiment.

For over a year, she had tried to make a paint that would not wear out. She wanted to do something big. And if she could just make the paint, she knew that everybody would treat her better.

But right now she couldn't work on her paint. She had to take the clothes from the washer. She wadded them up and tossed them into the dryer.

[1]

Oh, if she could just invent that paint that would not wear out! She began to think about how they would talk to her. Berta would smile and say, "You're so smart, Irma." Carl would say, "That Irma is a real inventor."

The bell on the dryer went "ding." Irma took the clothes from the dryer and folded them.

Now Irma was done for the day. She felt good as she left the room where the washer and dryer were. It was now nine o'clock at night. And Irma didn't have to be at work until seven o'clock in the morning. She would be able to work on her paint for at least two or three hours.

This was the time of day that Irma always looked forward to. The washing was done. Everybody else was watching TV, so they wouldn't bother her. Now Irma could go into her lab and do her thing.

[2]

1

A	B	C	D	E
fond	next	felt	mail	fell
food	neat	feet	meal	feel

2

oi

A	B
oil	soil
noise	pointed

3

dart   serve   around

kitchen   foolish   boarders

4

relatives   husband   tomorrow

recall   chores   pretzels   hammer

bench   clink   super   crazy   shelf

invisible   invented   sticky   nail

upstairs   rattled   unhappy   dent

5

Irma Makes Paint

As you may recall from the last Irma story, Irma was very unhappy. She worked all day in the cheese factory. When she got home, she had to fix meals for her boarders. Then she washed the clothes while they watched TV.

When we left Irma, she felt good because she was done with her chores for the day. She could now work on her paint. She went into her lab and closed the door. She could hear the others upstairs laughing.

"Go get the pretzels," Carl said to Berta. "Get them yourself, you bum."

[1]

Irma went to the jars of paint she had been working with. She wanted to see how hard the paint in each jar was. The paint had been drying for almost three days.

She tapped the paint in the first jar. It was not hard. There was a film of hard paint on top, but the paint under the film was still wet and sticky.

She tapped the paint in the next jar. It was pretty hard, but there was still some soft paint under the film on top.

Irma went to the last jar of paint. She tapped it. It was hard. She tapped it harder and harder. She could not dent it. It was super hard.

[1]

"Maybe I did it," she said to herself. "Maybe I invented a super hard paint."

She got a hammer and a nail. She held the point of the nail on the paint. Then she hit the other end of the nail with the hammer. The paint did not dent. She hit the nail harder. The nail began to bend, but still the paint did not dent.

"Irma," Herman called from upstairs, "where are the pretzels? How can we watch TV without pretzels?"

"I'll be right up there," she said.

[1]

Irma left the nail on the paint. She set the hammer down and went upstairs. She went to a shelf in the kitchen and got a box of pretzels. She handed the box to Herman and smiled. "Here they are," she said.

He rattled the box. "What do you call this?" he said. "This box is nearly empty. I must have told you a hundred times, we can't watch TV without pretzels."

"I'll get some more tomorrow," Irma said. Then she went downstairs to her lab. She said to herself, "I will test that super paint some more."

[1]

She looked around for the nail, but she could not see it. So she got another nail. She held the point of the nail on the paint, and then she stopped. She felt something on the paint. She could not see anything on the paint, but she could feel it. It felt like a nail.

She ran her finger over the point. It *was* a nail. It was the same nail that she had tested the paint with before. She could feel where it had bent. But she could not see the nail. It was invisible.

[1]

She picked it up and held it next to the light in the room. Still she could not see it. "Maybe I've been working too hard," she said. "Nails are not invisible."

But no matter what she said to herself, there she was, holding an invisible nail. She dropped it on the floor. "Clink," it went. It sounded like a nail. She felt around on the floor until she found it. It felt like a nail, but it didn't look like a nail. It didn't look like anything.

[1]

She picked up the nail and went to the work bench. She sat down on the work bench and said to herself, "I have to think this thing out. I left the nail on the paint in the last jar. When I came back, the nail had become invisible. Maybe . . ."

She was ready to think that maybe the paint in the jar had turned the nail into an invisible nail. But she was afraid to think that anything so crazy had happened. "Maybe . . . ," she said to herself. Then she said, "Oh. Maybe that paint turned the nail invisible."

Irma was afraid to test what she was thinking. She had wanted to make a paint that was super hard. She didn't even think that she would make a paint that made things invisible.

[2]

1

A	B	C	D	E
food	burn	benches	pointed	load
fold	barn	beaches	painted	loud

2

soiled   cooled   eaten   watched   pounded

3

listened   tests   invisible   copper

silver   glass   flatter   visible

grime   lazy   removes   relatives

freezer   stomped   floor

Irma Tests the Invisible Paint

Irma had left a nail on the hard paint. When she came back to her lab, the nail was invisible. Slowly she began to realize that the paint had made the nail invisible.

She said to herself, "I will test that paint." She took a coin from her purse and dropped the coin on the paint. Then she watched and waited. After a while, she saw that the coin was starting to turn invisible. It now looked like a glass coin. She could still see it, but it did not look like a copper coin or a silver coin. It looked like a glass coin.

[1]

She dropped it on the floor. "Clink," it went. It sounded like a coin. She took a hammer and hit the coin ten times. She wanted to see what would happen to it now. The coin got flatter and bigger, but it still looked like glass. She said, "I don't believe what is happening."

She set the coin on the paint again and waited. Soon the coin was invisible. Now it didn't look like glass. It didn't look like anything.

"I don't believe it," Irma said to herself. She felt the coin. She could feel the dents that had been made by the hammer.

[1]

Irma closed her eyes and picked up the coin. "It feels like it should feel," she said to herself. Then she opened her eyes and looked at the coin in her hand. It was invisible.

She said, "I must see how this invisible paint works." She got a pot of water and heated it on the stove in her lab. When the water began to boil, she dropped the coin into it. Then she watched to see what would happen.

Slowly she could see the coin begin to form at the bottom of the boiling water. Slowly it became visible. At first the coin looked like glass. Then it began to look like a coin that had been pounded with a hammer.

[1]

She lifted the coin from the boiling water and set it on a sheet of foil. When the coin had cooled, she picked it up and looked at it. She said, "I know that I can remove the invisible paint with boiling water. Now I will try something else."

She took a soiled rag and tore off a small bit. She set the bit of rag on the hard paint. Then she watched as the rag became invisible.

"Now I will see if something else will remove that invisible paint." She took the bit of soiled rag and dropped it in the washtub. Then she turned on the cold water and let it run over the rag.

[2]

The water washed away bits of grime. As each bit of grime left the rag, a spot became visible. But the rest of the rag was still invisible. "Cold water does not seem to work too well," Irma said.

Then she took a can of motor oil from the shelf. She filled a cup with oil and dropped the rag into the cup of oil. Slowly the rag became visible. Irma smiled. She said, "Oil removes the invisible paint."

Now Irma had to think. She could hardly believe what had happened. She went over everything five times. Then she shook her head and said, "It must have happened. I must have made a paint that turns things invisible."

[2]

"Irma," Berta called from upstairs, "what happened to that gallon of ice cream that was in the freezer?"

Irma said, "If it's not in the freezer, you must have eaten it."

Berta yelled, "Well, why didn't you get more? How can we watch TV if we don't have ice cream?"

Irma said, "You'll just have to do the best you can."

Berta did not say anything. She stomped back to the living room. As Irma listened to her lazy boarder walking across the floor, she got an idea. She smiled and said to herself, "I think I can have a lot of fun with this invisible paint."

[1]

1

<u>A</u>	<u>B</u>	<u>C</u>	<u>D</u>	<u>E</u>
boiling	coach	want	pond	clod
bailing	couch	went	pound	cloud

2

sp<u>oi</u>l   <u>l</u>urk   fl<u>oa</u>ting   ar<u>ou</u>nd   t<u>oo</u>l   ba<u>tch</u>

3

<u>voi</u>ce   recall   invisible   wat<u>ched</u>
stinky   mirror   cracked   chairs   else
easy   spun   Fern   women   while
smiled   dumped   waved
window   listened

Irma Gives Them a Hand

As you may recall, Irma had made a batch of invisible paint. Then she got an idea about how she could have a lot of fun with that paint.

She began to think of all kinds of fun things that she could do. She could rub the paint on herself. Then she could go upstairs and pay back her boarders for being mean to her. She could scare them. She could play jokes on them. She smiled to herself as she began to think about the things she could do.

"Irma," Herman yelled. "We are trying to move the couch. Get up here and <u>give</u> us a hand."

"Yes," Irma answered. "I'll give you a hand."

[1]

Quickly she grabbed the jar with the invisible paint in it. She dumped the paint from the jar. Then she began rubbing the paint on herself. She rubbed it on her head, her arms, her body, her legs, and her feet. She rubbed paint on every part of her but her right hand. Then she waited and watched as she became invisible.

"Irma, get up here and give us a hand. You can fool around in that stinky basement some other time."

Irma looked at herself in the cracked mirror that was in her lab. "Oh, dear," she said. She had not painted her eyes. There they were, two eyes staring into the mirror. "This will spoil the trick," she said. "What can I do to make my eyes invisible?"

[2]

"I've got it," she said to herself. She went to a shelf and found an old pair of sun glasses. She rubbed the paint on the glasses.

"Irma, get up here right now," Herman called. "When I say that I need a hand, I want you to come right now."

"Yes," Irma said. She picked up the glasses and slipped them on. Then she looked in the mirror again. No eyes looked back at her.

She smiled and looked down at her right hand. It seemed to be floating in the air. She waved at the mirror. "Wow," she said. "This is really a kick."

[1]

"Irma, get up here right now!" Herman called.

So Irma went upstairs. And as she walked up the stairs, she said to herself, "So you wanted me to give you a hand. I'll do that. I will give you a hand."

She walked into the living room. Herman was standing in front of the TV set. Berta and Herman's brother were sitting in chairs. Carl was saying, "Herman, sit down. We can't see a thing when you're standing in front of the TV."

Fern, one of the women from the third floor, was facing the window, looking out. She was saying, "Oh, all we ever do is watch TV. Why don't we ever do anything else?"

[1]

As they talked, a man on TV was saying, "Yes, we have the best—the very best—cars in town. Come down today. If you don't have any cash, come anyhow. We'll fix you up. We'll fix you good."

In a loud voice, Irma said, "You wanted me to give you a hand?"

Herman spun around. "Who said that?" he asked. "That sounded like Irma. Irma, was that you?"

Berta said, "I don't know why we stay here. She is all for herself. She never thinks about anybody else."

[1]

Again Irma talked. "Here is the hand you wanted," she said and held up her right hand.

Berta looked at the hand. Her eyes became very big. Her mouth dropped open. Her lips moved, but she did not say anything.

Herman looked at the hand, too. And his mouth fell open. His lips moved, but his voice did not seem to be working.

Carl looked, too. "Uh, buh, duh, buh, buh, uh," he said. His voice was working—but not too well.

Then Fern turned away from the window. She started to say, "We don't even go out to eat any more. We don't . . ." She stopped talking and stared at the hand.

[2]

1

A	B	C	D	E
fail	painted	seal	brother	boast
foil	parted	sell	bother	boost

2

dreams faintcd hurry
cheeks muttered float

3

nice face voice track chuckle really
ready limp tank important soaked
except buh duh sense shower

4

Did They Really Want a Hand?

Irma had come up to give Herman and the others a hand. She had made every part of herself invisible except her right hand. She went to the living room. Then she said, "You wanted a hand? Here it is." She waved the hand around.

The others stopped and stared. They were still staring. The man on the TV was saying, "Yes, friends, we have a car for everybody. So come on down to the Car Mart and pick out the car of your dreams."

Carl was still saying, "Buh, duh, uh, buh, buh, uh, duh." Then he stopped going, "Buh, duh," and started to say something else. "I'm getting out of . . . I'm getting . . . I'm . . ."

[1]

Suddenly Carl turned around and took a dive at the window. "Crash," the glass went, and Carl went rolling on the ground outside the window. He got up and ran. He ran like a streak. "I'm getting out of . . . I'm getting . . . ," he yelled.

Berta stood there and stared at the hand for a while. Then she said, "Is that hand a hand, or is that hand not a hand? Or is . . . ?"

Irma said, "You wanted me to give you a hand, didn't you?"

"Yes, yes, a hand," Berta said. "Yes, thank you. Thank you very much for the hand. Thank you. That was very nice." Her face had turned white. "That was very, very nice."

[1]

Irma said, "Now, what do you want this hand for?"

Berta said, "Oh. Well, I mean—just keep the hand right there, and I'll be right back."

Berta started to walk from the room. Then she began to run. She ran as fast as a track star. Out the front door she went. She didn't yell anything. She just ran.

Irma started to chuckle. Then she turned to Herman. "I don't understand you," she said. "You said that you wanted a hand. What do you want to do with the hand?"

"Well, you see . . . ," he said. "Well, when I said that I needed a hand, I didn't really mean that I wanted a hand. What I wanted was a hand. You know. I didn't want a hand. I wanted a hand."

[2]

"Herman," Irma said, "you're not making much sense."

"Ohhhhhh," said Fern. She fainted and fell like a limp rag on the floor.

The man on the TV was saying, "These cars won't last, so hurry down. Come on down right now, and we'll give you a free tank of gas."

Herman was saying, "Well, I think I had better go now. You see, I have to . . . I mean there's a man who is waiting to see me, and I . . . It's very important. And I . . ." Suddenly he stopped talking and dashed out the front door.

[1]

Irma began to laugh. "That was fun," she said. "That was really a lot of fun." She sat down on the floor and laughed. She laughed until her sides hurt. She laughed until invisible tears ran down her invisible cheeks.

Fern woke up while Irma was still laughing. She muttered, "I must have had a bad dream. I must . . ."

Irma was next to her on the floor. Irma said, "If you don't want a hand, how would you like some teeth?" Irma opened her mouth and showed her teeth. They were not invisible.

Fern looked at the teeth and passed out again.

[1]

Irma laughed some more. Then she said, "I had better go downstairs now and get rid of this invisible paint."

She ran down the stairs and into her lab. She took off the glasses and tossed them on the work bench. She grabbed a rag and soaked it in oil. Then she rubbed the rag on the invisible paint. Slowly she became very visible again.

Then she said, "I'd better go upstairs and take a shower to get rid of this oil." So she did. Then she slipped into a clean dress, fixed her hair, and went back to the living room.

Fern was just waking up again. "Hello, Fern," Irma said.

Fern muttered, "I can see you. I can . . ." Then she fainted again.

[2]

1

dove carry movie place
knock face creeps tie
shrugged inside remarked

2

offering closed doesn't
shotgun sale drapes flipped
floating problem off realize
shower pale stared started

3

Looking for the Hand

After Irma had given Herman and the others a "hand," she removed the invisible paint with oil. Then she took a shower and went back to the living room. When Fern saw her, she passed out again.

Irma laughed and walked over to the TV set. The same man was still on the TV. He was saying, "Before we return to the movie, let me just show you three or four more of the cars that we are offering as part of our sale."

Irma turned off the set. Then she closed the drapes on the window that had been broken when Carl dove out. Then Irma sat down and began to think of other things that she could do.

[2]

At last, Fern woke up. She was very pale. She sat up and stared at Irma. Then she started to say, "Are you really . . . ?"

Just then Carl came in the front door. "Where is that hand?" he asked. He was carrying a shotgun.

Irma held out her hand. "Here it is," she said.

"Not that hand," Carl said. "I want the hand that was floating around this room."

Irma pointed to her hand. "This is it," she said.

"Come on, Irma," Carl said. "This is no time to fool around."

[1]

Fern ran over to Carl and stood next to him. She said, "This place gives me the creeps. Let's get out of here."

"Not until I find that hand," Carl said.

Suddenly a knock came from the front door. "See who that is," Carl said to Fern.

"See who it is yourself," she said.

"I'll see who it is," Irma said. She opened the door.

Two cops were standing next to Herman. One cop said, "Does this man live here?"

"Yes, he does," Irma said.

The cop said, "I think he's flipped. All he talks about is some hand that is floating around his living room."

[1]

Irma said, "Herman doesn't lie. If he says that he saw a hand, he saw a hand."

The cop said, "Well, something's funny. Do you want us to lock him up?"

"No, no," Irma said. "I think that he'll be all right."

The cop looked at Herman. Herman did not look very well. Then the cop looked at the other cop and said, "What do you think? Do you think this bird is safe?"

The other cop shrugged. "It's their problem. If they want him, they can have him."

"He's yours," the first cop said, and she led Herman into the hall.

[1]

Herman just stood there staring into the living room. " 'I'll give you a hand,' it said. And then I saw the hand. It was just floating in the air. And I saw it . . ."

"You'll be all right, Herman," Irma said.

The cops left, and Irma led Herman into the living room. He sat down on the couch and began to stare at the TV set. He didn't seem to realize that the set was turned off.

As the cops were leaving, Berta came running up the front walk. She grabbed one of the cops and said, "Come with me. You've got to come with me. There's a hand in our living room. It's just floating around. It's a hand, I tell you. It's a hand floating in the air."

"Here we go again," the first cop remarked.

[2]

The other cop said, "We're going to have to keep an eye on this place. There seems to be something funny going on here."

"Don't say I'm lying," Berta shouted. "When I say I saw a hand, I saw a hand. Come inside and I'll show it to you."

"No thanks," the first cop said. "We've just been in there, and we didn't see any hands floating around."

The cops led Berta inside. She pointed to the living room. "Where is it?" she asked. "It's not here."

Irma said, "It's all right, Berta, just sit down."

[1]

1

A	B	C	D	E
hunt	beet	star	set	bold
hurt	belt	stare	sit	bald

2

normal   bounding   nerve   hardens
broiling   starved   complaining   batch

3

wouldn't   again   bothering   dazed
helping   evenings   kitchen   bedroom
bathroom   tacos   grunted   basement
listen   chore   remarked   stomped
second   careful   face
remember   factory   carry   knock

4

Irma Gets Ready

After Irma had scared Carl and the other boarders with the hand, she made up her mind about two things.

The first thing was that she wouldn't scare them again, unless they were mean to her.

The second was that she would make another batch of paint, a big batch.

For the next three or four days, everyone was pretty nice to Irma. They weren't really nice. They just weren't bothering her as much as they had. In fact, they didn't say much. They seemed to be dazed.

[1]

Before Irma had scared them, Carl had eaten like a goat. But now he wouldn't even finish one helping. Before Herman had been scared, he had spent more time complaining than eating. But now he just picked at his food without saying much.

And after dinner, Fern and Berta went into the living room and sat. Sometimes they would not remember to turn on the TV set. They just sat and stared at the set.

Irma got a lot done on these days. Right after dinner, she would go down to the lab and work on her paint. She boiled sheep fat. The smell was bad, but nobody yelled, "Stop making that stink down there."

[1]

Irma mixed in a little of this and a little of that. Then she mixed the paint. The first batch didn't work. Irma must have done something that wasn't right. "This batch is spoiled," she said.

Then she began to boil another batch. She was very careful. For two evenings she toiled over that batch. But it worked. When she was done, she had five gallons of invisible paint.

She left most of the paint in a big pot. But she also filled three broiling pans with the rest of it. She said to herself, "When the paint in these pans hardens, I will have so much invisible paint that I'll be able to make everything in this house invisible if I want to."

[2]

Irma hid one of the pans in the kitchen. She hid the second pan in her bedroom. She hid the third pan in the bathroom. The rest of the paint stayed in her lab.

Five days after Irma had scared the others, things seemed to get back to normal in Irma's house. When she came home from the cheese factory, Herman met her at the door. "Where have you been?" he asked. "Don't you know what time it is? What do you mean by coming home so late?"

Berta was standing behind Herman. She was saying, "We're starved. Where are the tacos? And I hope they are not too hot. You know I can't stand hot tacos."

Irma said, "Berta, there was a big line at the taco place. I'm sorry, but I went there right from work."

[2]

Herman grunted something and stomped into the kitchen. As Irma walked inside the house, Carl came bounding out of the living room. "I can't stand the smell in this house any more. Get rid of that junk you're working with in the basement."

Irma stopped in the hall. She said, "I have something to say."

Herman came out of the kitchen and said, "Say it later. Just get that junk on the table and let's eat."

"No," Irma said. "I have something to say, and I'm going to say it right now. And I want all of you to listen."

[1]

"All right, all right," Carl said. "Say what you have to say. Just make it fast."

Irma said, "From now on, don't yell at me. Don't tell me to do every chore around this house. And don't be mean to me."

Berta said, "Who do you think you are, talking to me in that tone of voice?"

"You know very well who I am," Irma said. "Just remember what I'm telling you."

"Oh, be quiet, and let's eat," Carl remarked.

[1]

1

A	B	C	D	E
soil	cold	first	clean	these
sail	cool	fist	clear	those

2

A	B	C
ce	ice	face
ci	nice	circle
	race	place

4

A	B
down	downstairs
pocket	pocketbook
up	upstairs

3

nerve   meanest   chomping
offering   lousy   stealing

5

quiet   warned   carried
clever   glasses   savings
pretzels   cooled   cola   keys
wise   taco   stomped   nobody
listen   bugging   loudly

6

A Chunk of Ice Down the Back

Irma had warned the others. But they didn't take her warning. They yelled at her and told her that she had a lot of nerve for talking to them that way.

Irma did not fight with them. She sat and ate her taco while they yelled at her. Then she cleaned up the kitchen while they went into the living room, and when they were watching TV, she went downstairs.

She was pretty mad. At first she wanted to do the meanest thing she could think of. But she sat and cooled off for a while. Then she said, "I must think of a plan that is clever."

[1]

After thinking for a while, she said, "I've got it." She got a pick and a hammer. She broke a chunk of paint from the pot of invisible paint. She began to rub the paint on every part of her. Then she slipped the invisible glasses on and went upstairs.

Irma was thinking, "They yell at me so much that they don't have time to fight with each other. I will fix that."

She went to Carl's room. She felt in the pockets of Carl's coat. She found his car keys. She carried the keys into the living room. She walked behind Herman. He was chomping on pretzels and watching TV.

[1]

Irma slipped Carl's keys into Herman's back pocket. Then she picked up Herman's glass of cola. She set the glass on a table next to Carl. Then she took a chunk of ice from the glass and dropped it down the back of Berta's dress.

Berta shot off of the couch. "Wwwwoooo," she screamed. Then she turned to Carl, who was sitting next to her. "What's the big idea?" she screamed.

Carl said, "What's bugging you?"

"You dropped a chunk of ice down my dress!" she yelled. "And I don't think you're one bit funny."

[1]

"What ice?" Carl said. "I don't have any ice. I don't even have a glass."

"What do you call that on the table next to you?" she yelled. She was pointing at the glass that Irma had taken from Herman.

Irma started to laugh. But nobody could hear her because they were yelling so loudly.

Herman was yelling, "That's my glass. What's the big idea of stealing my glass?"

Carl was saying, "I don't know how that glass got there. I didn't take it."

Berta was screaming, "Are you telling us that the glass just jumped over there by itself? Are you trying to tell us that the chunk of ice just jumped down my back all by itself?"

[2]

One of the other boarders yelled, "Will you all be quiet! I'm trying to watch TV."

And the man on TV was saying, "Yes, we still have some of last year's cars that we are offering—right now—at a savings that you won't believe."

Finally Carl said, "I don't know what's going on here, but I'm not taking any more. I'm getting out."

He stomped out of the living room. He grabbed his coat from the closet. He slipped into it. He reached into his pocket for his keys. "All right," he said. "Who is the wise one?"

[1]

"What's the matter with you?" Herman said to Carl.

"Just give me my keys back, and I'll get out of here."

"What are you talking about?" Herman said.

"Who has my keys?" Carl yelled. "Give them back right now. They were right here in my pocket, and some wise one lifted them."

Fern yelled, "Will you cut the noise! I can't even hear what they're saying on TV."

The man on TV said, "Come and look at these fine cars. We have one that is just made for your pocketbook."

Carl was yelling, "I want my keys."

Berta was yelling, "I hope you can find them, so you can get out of here, you bum."

Herman was yelling, "I don't know anything about your lousy keys."

And Irma was laughing.

[2]

1

<u>A</u>	<u>B</u>	<u>C</u>
ce	rice	placed
ci	ice	city

2

<u>chunk</u> <u>noise</u> <u>tooth</u>
<u>outside</u> <u>coins</u> <u>shirt</u>

3

<u>few</u> sure <u>wearing</u> <u>liar</u> swipe
punch yourself stick pizza
mouth quite quiet socked
slipped aside warned carried
removed front hungry who

4

The Big Fight

Irma had done some things to start a fight between her boarders. She had removed Carl's keys from his coat and slipped them into Herman's pocket. She had taken a glass and placed it next to Carl. Then she had taken a chunk of ice from the glass and dropped it down Berta's back.

Now everybody was yelling. Carl was yelling because he couldn't find his keys. Berta was yelling because of the ice down her back. Fern was yelling because the others were making so much noise that she couldn't watch TV. And Herman was yelling because Carl was yelling at him about <u>the</u> keys.

[1]

All at once Herman stood up. "Come on," he said to Carl. "If you think I've got your keys, look in my pockets. Come on."

"All right, I will," Carl said.

"No, you won't," Herman said. "Just keep your hands to yourself. I'll show you what's in my pockets."

Herman took some coins from his front pocket. "There," he said. "Do those look like your keys?" Then he took some folding money from another pocket. "Maybe you think that these are yours, too?" Then Herman took the keys from his back pocket. He held them up and said, "The next thing you know, you'll be telling me that these are your keys."

"They *are* my keys," Carl said.

[2]

Herman looked at the keys. Then he looked at Carl. Then he shrugged. "How did these get in my pocket?" he asked.

Carl said, "You don't have any idea, do you? You didn't take them from my coat, did you? You didn't swipe them, did you?"

"No, I didn't," Herman said. "And if you want to make something out of it, step outside, and I'll show you who is a liar."

"You're a liar, that's who," Carl said.

Herman ran at Carl, but Carl stepped aside and Herman hit the wall. "Ow," he yelled. Carl laughed and while he was laughing, Herman hit him in the nose.

[2]

Then Carl hit Herman, and they both went down on the floor. Carl socked Herman in the mouth and knocked a tooth out.

And while they were fighting, Fern was yelling, "Will you stop that? Go outside if you want to fight."

And the man on TV was saying, "You can save big money on these cars."

The next day was a very quiet day. When Irma got home from work, nobody yelled at her. Carl had a black eye. He wasn't talking to Herman because they had had a fight. He wasn't talking to Berta because she wasn't talking to him.

Berta was not talking to Carl because she was sure that he had dropped the ice down her back. She wasn't talking to Herman because he hadn't stuck up for her.

[2]

Herman wasn't talking because he had a tooth missing. He was afraid that everybody would laugh at him if he opened his mouth.

So all was quiet. After work Irma came home with pizza. She said, "Hello," and everybody nodded. She asked Herman, "How does your mouth feel today?"

He said, "Mmm, mmmm." He didn't want to open his mouth.

She said to Carl, "And how are you today?"

He said, "Yes, right."

She said to Fern, "I got the biggest pizza for our dinner."

Fern said, "I'm not hungry."

[1]

1

A	B	C	D
beach	shout	burn	soil
bench	shoot	barn	sail

2

dealing   whiter   bother   circle   face

shower   tonight   roller   complaining

3

trouble   false   mood   suddenly

upstairs   dentist's   rolled   liar

dazed   forget   few   wearing

quiet   floor   socked   flying

another   sure   followed

4

Another Big Fight

After Irma had given the others a hand, they had been quiet for a few days. After she made them fight among themselves, they were quiet again. But on the third day after the fight, Herman began to complain again. He was mad because he had to go to the dentist. He complained about the dentist's bill for his false tooth. He shouldn't have complained, because Irma loaned him the money to pay the dentist's bill.

Two days later, everybody was complaining again. They complained because Irma came home with hamburgers. "Hamburgers again?" they moaned. "Oh, I can't stand hamburgers."

[1]

Irma said, "Remember what happened last time? If you're mean to me, I'll be mean to you."

"Oh, be quiet and let's eat," Herman said. His false tooth was whiter than his other teeth.

"Okay," she remarked. "Just remember what I said."

Everybody yelled at Irma as they ate. So after dinner Irma went down to her lab. She wasn't in the mood to rub invisible paint all over herself. She didn't mind rubbing the paint on so much. But it was a bother to get the paint off. First she had to rub herself with oil. Then she had to take a shower. That was a lot of trouble.

[1]

Suddenly she had a good idea. She fumbled around on the work bench until she found the invisible glasses. Then she took them upstairs. Berta was sitting in the living room chair. She was sound asleep. So Irma slipped the glasses on Berta. Then Irma left the room and waited.

Pretty soon Fern walked into the living room. She said, "I'm getting tired of watching the late show. I think I'll watch the roller game tonight." Then she looked at Berta.

[1]

Berta didn't look as if she were wearing glasses. She looked as if she had two big holes in her head. You could see the back of the chair by looking into the glasses. And when Fern took one look into the glasses, she said, "Ohhh," and fainted.

And when Herman walked into the room, he saw Fern on the floor. He said, "What's going on here?" Then he said, "Berta, what happened to Fern?" He was still looking at Fern. Then he said, "Berta, what happened?"

He looked up. Then his eyes rolled around, and he fainted, too.

Irma ran into the room and took the glasses from Berta's face.

Herman was still out like a light, but Fern woke up. She looked at Berta. "Oooh!" she said.

[2]

Just then, Herman woke up. He reached over and grabbed Fern. He began to say, "She has holes in her head. She has . . ."

Just then Carl walked in. "What's going on in here?" he said, looking at Fern and Herman on the floor.

Herman said, "It's Berta. She has holes in her head."

Fern said, "That's right. She doesn't have any eyes."

Carl looked at Berta. Then he said to Herman, "So you're on the floor because Berta has holes in her head. Is that right?"

"That's right," Herman said.

[1]

Carl said, "Well, stand up, Herman. I want to show you something you haven't seen before."

Herman was dazed. He stood up. Then he asked, "What do you want to show me?"

"This," Carl said. He socked Herman in the mouth. Herman's false tooth went flying across the room.

A big fight followed. When it was over, Herman had two teeth missing. Carl had two black eyes. Fern had one black eye.

And Berta had a good sleep. When she woke up, she looked around the room at the mess. "What happened?" she asked.

All of the others said, "Forget it!"

[2]

1

A	B	C	D	E
check	pick	tell	shot	spill
cheek	pack	tall	shoot	spell

2

price   circus   except   peace
certain   twice   face   nice

3

worth   you'll   we'd   paying   smiled
whistled   simmering   stove   spilling
doctor   checked   uncle's   quite   blush
trailers   slipped   cola   sixth   fifth
trouble   once   few   false   quiet
warned   supper   scared

4

Things Get Better

Irma didn't like the idea of paying for two more false teeth, but she said to herself, "I think it's worth the price." One of Herman's false teeth did not fit quite right. And when he said words with an *s* in them, he whistled. He could say, "What are we having for dinner?" without whistling. But when he said, "I smell something simmering on the stove," he sounded like a bird.

For two weeks after the last fight nobody yelled at Irma. By now Herman had two new false teeth. Carl's black eyes were almost gone. And Fern's black eye was almost gone.

[1]

For two weeks everybody seemed tired of fighting. But then it started up again. Everybody began to pick on Irma. And Irma warned them. She pointed her finger at them and said, "If you give me a hard time, I will see to it that you get a hard time right back."

They told her to shut up.

That night she put the invisible glasses on their cat and let the cat walk through the living room. Berta passed out. Herman saw the cat and spilled his glass of cola on Carl. Carl did not see the cat. He got mad at Herman for spilling the cola on him. A big fight started.

[1]

After the fight Herman had three teeth missing. Carl had two black eyes. And Fern had to go to a doctor to get her eyes checked. When she told the doctor about the cat with two holes in its head, the doctor said that she needed a rest. So she went to her uncle's place and stayed there for two weeks.

Things were quiet again, except for the whistling of Herman's three false teeth. But they didn't whistle too often because Herman didn't talk too much. Once in a while he would say something like, "Are we having tacos for supper again?" But then his teeth would whistle so much that he would blush and not say anything for a long time.

[2]

When Fern came back, everybody started yelling at Irma again. This time she got back at them by rubbing paint on her long robe. Then she slipped into the robe and walked into the living room.

The man on TV was saying, "We'll take anything in trade for these fine cars. We'll trade for boats, goats. We'll trade for house trailers, mouse traps. . . ."

Irma walked into the living room. She stood in front of the TV set. "How do you like my new robe?" she asked.

Everybody looked at the robe, but they couldn't see it. They could see the man on TV. And they could see Irma's feet and her head and her hands. But that is all they could see.

[2]

Berta was sleeping. Carl spilled his cola on her. Herman jumped out of the window. Fern said something about an eye doctor and fainted again.

And so it went. Every time Irma's boarders were mean to her, she got even with them. But they got mad at her less often. The first time she scared them, they were mean after five days. The next time, they didn't pick on her for a week. The next time, they didn't pick on her for two weeks. And the fifth time she got even with them, they didn't pick on her for over three months.

[1]

Irma's boarders didn't bother her. They didn't yell. They didn't complain. They seemed to be tired of fighting. In fact, Herman was even nice to her from time to time. One time she came home late with a pizza. Carl started to say something about how late she was, and Herman said, "Listen here. She works in that cheese factory all day and still brings us dinner. So stop complaining."

He whistled seven times when he said that. But it made Irma feel very good.

Irma smiled at Herman and said, "Well, thank you, Herman. That was a very nice thing for you to say."

And Herman even smiled.

[1]

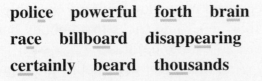

1

police   powerful   forth   brain
race   billboard   disappearing
certainly   beard   thousands

2

audience   magician   stage   world
begun   crooks   spies   banker
fantastic   bottom   presto   people   woman
blanket   once   word   trouble   worth

3

Things Get Very Good

When Irma had begun working in her lab, she had hoped that she would make a super hard paint. She had hoped that she would become rich and powerful. But instead of inventing a super hard paint, she had invented a paint that made things invisible. And now she wasn't too sure about telling anybody about her paint.

Here's how she saw it: If she told people about the paint, she would make a lot of money. But who would want to use the paint? Crooks would like to use it. They could rub the paint on themselves and rob banks. And nobody would be safe if that paint got on the market. You wouldn't be able to tell when somebody was in the room with you. [1]

When you walked down the street at night, you wouldn't know when an invisible hand might reach out and grab you. The crooks would love the invisible paint, but the cops would hate it. Spies would love it. Bankers would hate it. Con men would love it. People with cash in their pockets would hate it.

Irma did a lot of thinking about her paint. From time to time she told herself, "I don't care how people use this paint. I can get a lot of money for it. I won't have to work in the cheese factory when I sell my paint." [1]

But then another part of her brain would say, "Irma you can't do that. It isn't right."

Then the different parts of her brain would begin to say things back and forth until Irma would shake her head. She would say, "Stop! I can't think about it anymore." But later she would think about it again. And again the different parts of her mind would say things back and forth.

Then one day—one very hot day—Irma made up her mind. She said, "I will not let anybody have my paint. I will keep my paint, but I will use it only when I have to use it. I will not tell anybody about it, not even Herman."

[1]

Irma felt that it was a shame not to let others know about her paint, but she felt that it was best this way. Besides, things were going pretty well at the boarding house. By the middle of the summer, Herman was no longer picking on Irma. In fact, he was sticking up for her. From time to time Berta would start to gripe about Irma. When this happened, Herman would say, "Stop griping, Berta. She's a good woman."

And one day late in the summer, Carl and Fern said that they were leaving. Irma was glad to see them leave. They seemed glad about leaving, too.

[1]

After Fern and Carl had gone, Herman said, "It's so nice and quiet without them around this place." He whistled five times when he said that.

Irma was beginning to think that she had no more use for the invisible paint. But then one day when she was walking home from the hamburger place, she saw a billboard. On it was the face of a man with a beard. "Arnold, the Best Magician in the World," it said on the billboard.

[1]

Irma stared at the billboard. Then she snapped her fingers. "That's it!" she said. "I'll become a magician. With my invisible paint, I'll be able to do tricks that nobody has ever been able to do before."

And that's just what happened. Maybe you have seen her. She is called "Irma the Fantastic." And she is fantastic. She gets into a big box, and they saw her into two parts. Lots of magicians do this trick. But when Irma the Fantastic does it, the bottom part of her gets out and walks around. Then the bottom part gets into the box again, and—presto—out comes Irma.

[1]

She does many tricks, but the one that people come from all over to see is her disappearing trick. She stands in the middle of the stage. Then she rubs a magic cloth over herself. As everybody watches her, she begins to disappear. At first she looks as if she is made of glass. But pretty soon she is gone.

She lies down on the stage and Herman (who works with her) throws a blanket over her. The blanket shows the form of her body. But when he jerks the blanket away, nothing is there—except her voice. She talks to the people in the audience while she is invisible.

Other magicians have offered her thousands and thousands of dollars to show them how to do that trick, but Irma is keeping her word. She won't tell anybody about the invisible paint.

[2]

1

A	B	C	D	E
truck	packed	farther	stared	spell
trunk	parked	further	started	spill

2

Salt sailor South themselves
Pacific white forty cargo
chests officer spoil match loudly

3

captain bridge Rosa war
treasure younger great break
audience sunk hidden front
retired mumble listened world
tales Atlantic poke North
South relatives America Tony
twenty yakking workers worth

4

Old Salt, the Retired Sailor

They called him Old Salt, and they liked to make fun of him. Old Salt was a retired sailor. They didn't hate him. They didn't really think that they were being mean to him. They just liked to make him mad. So when they went past his house on their way to school, they would call to him, "Hey, Old Salt. Have you found your ship yet? Hey—Salt! Let's go hunting for treasures."

"Be on your way," Old Salt would holler from his window. "What do you know about hidden treasures?"

"Come on, Salt," the kids would yell. "Let's go hunting for treasures."

"Be on your way," Salt would yell. Then he'd mumble to himself and the kids would laugh.

[1]

When Old Salt had first moved into that little white house a year before, the girls and boys hadn't made fun of him. They listened to Old Salt tell about his days as a first officer on cargo ships. They heard him tell about the First World War and about the Second World War. They listened to his tales about a chest of gold that had been taken from the SS *Foil* just before it had gone down in the South Pacific.

The old man told the boys and girls that the *Foil* had sunk in 1918, while World War I was going on.

[1]

"Yes, kids," he had told them. "I saw the map that showed where they hid that gold. A funny map it was. Everything was in a code with numbers and letters."

At the time the kids had listened with wide eyes. But later they asked each other, "Did you believe that stuff about the hidden treasure?"

"Not me," they all said. "Old Salt just likes to talk."

The kids loved to listen to Old Salt tell about the roaring North Atlantic Sea in the middle of winter and about how the sea would break ships apart just the way you would break matchsticks. They loved to hear about parts of South America and the things that happened there.

[1]

But they would not admit that they loved to listen to the old man. That's why they began to make fun of him. They made fun of him so that nobody would know that they really liked him. They were really mad at themselves for liking him.

So they called to him every day on their way to school. And every day he'd poke his head out of the window. He'd shake his fist and yell, "Be on your way." But then one day something happened that changed a lot of things for Old Salt and two of the kids.

[1]

On that day a truck was parked in front of Old Salt's house. Two workers were carrying a big trunk up the front steps. Salt was holding the door open for them.

Tony, a sixteen-year-old boy who lived on the block, was on his way to school with his fifteen-year-old sister, Rosa.

"Hey, Salt," Tony yelled. "What's in the trunk?"

"Be on your way," he snapped.

"Come on, Salt. Tell us really. What's in the trunk?"

" 'Tis the things left behind by the best captain that ever sailed a ship."

"What do you mean?" Tony asked.

"My captain is dead. And a sad day it was when he died. He has no relatives. So they're sending his things to me."

[2]

"What's in that chest?" Rosa asked.

"A sailor's life is in this chest. Forty years of toil are in this chest. The dreams of a great man are in this chest."

"Hey, buddy," one of the workers from the truck said. "Will you stop yakking and just hold the door open so we can get this junk inside?"

"Junk, is it?" Old Salt said. "If I were twenty years younger—" Salt shook his fist at the worker.

The worker said, "If you were twenty years younger, you'd still be an old man."

Tony said, "Hey, Salt, can I look at the stuff in that trunk sometime?"

Salt stared at Tony. Salt was trying to see if Tony was going to make fun of him.

[2]

1

A	B	C	D
limp	punch	toil	truck
lamp	pouch	tail	trunk

2

dance　place　chill　Saint's
chest　Pacific　decide　finger
officer　chance　twice

3

A	B
bed	bedroom
out	outside
down	downstairs

4

uniforms　pictures　close　knock
kidding　limp　medal　brass
bong　ashamed　magnifying　dead
yeah　ah　code　treasure　younger

5

The Captain's Chest

A truck was parked in front of Old Salt's house. Salt was holding the door open for the two workers who were carrying a big trunk into the house. Tony had asked if they could look at the stuff in the trunk.

Salt stared at Tony. He was trying to see if Tony was going to make fun of him.

Tony said, "I'm not kidding, Salt. I'd really like to see what's in it."

Salt turned away. Without looking at Tony, he said, "Come around. Come around some time, and we'll see what we'll see."

Rosa yelled, "Yeah, Salt. Maybe it's a treasure."

"Knock it off," Tony said. "Don't make fun of him all the time. That stuff gets old after a while."

[1]

After school Tony said to Rosa, "Hey, let's go over to Old Salt's place and see what's in that trunk."

Rosa shook her head. "No, I don't think so." Then she shrugged. "Well, why not? Let's go."

So they went to Old Salt's place. They knocked on the door. They could hear Salt walking to the door. He walked with a limp. He opened the door. He stared at them.

"Come to make fun of my captain, have you? Well, let me tell you. Me, you can make fun of, but there won't be a word of fun made about my captain."

Tony said, "We won't make fun, Salt. We just want to see what's in the trunk."

[1]

"Come with me, then," Salt said. Then he led them up the stairs. Then he led them down the hall. There were pictures on the wall. Most of them showed sailors and ships. When Salt came to a door near the end of the hall, he stopped. "My captain's things are in here," he said.

Then he opened the door. The trunk was on the floor. It was open. Salt had taken some of the things from the trunk and placed them on the bed. There were a few medals. There was a big brass bell and a ship's clock. There were two uniforms, one of them with holes in it. There was the ship's log, and there were stacks of papers. Most of the papers were letters.

[1]

Tony looked at the captain's things, and he felt sad. Before he had come up the stairs, he had wanted to see everything in the trunk, but now he felt a little ashamed of even looking at the captain's things. Tony felt as if he were looking at things that he shouldn't see. Tony felt as if he were spying on the dead captain.

Rosa went over and hit the bell with her finger. "Bong," it sounded.

"Ah, that's a good sound," Old Salt said.

Rosa picked up a stack of letters. "Why did he save these letters?" she asked.

The old man grabbed the letters. "Don't be nosing around those," he snapped.

[1]

When he grabbed the letters, the string that bound them together broke, and some of the letters fell on the floor. "Now you've done it," Salt said.

"I didn't do that," Rosa said. "I was just holding onto them when you tore them out of my hand."

Tony bent down and began to help the old man pick up the letters. Tony picked up five or six letters and then he stopped. He was holding a small map, or something that looked like a map. It must have been in one of those letters. The map was covered with numbers and letters.

[1]

"Salt," Tony said, "what is this?"

Salt could not see very well without his glasses. He bent close to the paper. Then he said, "Saints be with us! It's the map, it is. It's the map of the *Foil* treasure!"

Tony felt a chill run up his back and grab him right behind the ears. That chill held onto him until his back was stiff. He stared at the map. Rosa stared at the map.

The old man ran over to a dresser and got a large magnifying glass from it. He laid the map down on the dresser top and held the glass close to his eyes. "Ah, it's the *Foil* map all right, with all of those letters on it."

[2]

Then Salt folded up the map and slipped it into his pocket. He patted the outside of his pocket and said, "This old sailor is going to be rich yet, he is."

Tony said, "Do you know where the treasure is?"

"It's all on this map," Salt said. "All I need to do is find out how the code works, and I'll know all there is to know."

Then Salt led Tony and Rosa downstairs. "Be off with you. Old Salt has a lot of work to do."

[1]

1

able   periods   arrows   island
window   inside   sure   nine
beyond   shook   yeah   puddles
compass   chance   sense   during
unfold   broken   specks

2

spell   crack   numbers   dotted   code
thousands   head   nine   really   ready
people   again   treasure   great   once
few   because   coming

3

Cracking the Code

Tony and Rosa didn't see Salt for over a week. Salt was inside working on the code. Nine days after the trunk had arrived at Salt's house, Tony saw Salt outside. It was a warm day. It had just rained, and puddles of water were on the ground. Salt was sitting on his front steps.

"Hello," Tony said. "How are you coming with the code on the *Foil* map?"

Salt shook his head. "Ah," he said, "that sure is a hard one. Worked day and night, I have. And still I can't make heads nor tails out of it. I think it is beyond me."

[1]

"Maybe you need some help," Tony said. "What if I helped you work on the code?"

Salt shook his head. "I don't know about that." His eyes looked at Tony. Then they looked down. "It might be that you could help."

"I'm ready," Tony said. "Let's take a look at that map."

Just then Rosa came down the street on her bike. She stopped and said, "Am I missing out on something?"

"Yeah," Tony said. "We're going to work on the code. Salt hasn't broken it yet."

[1]

Salt said, "Hold on. I don't want everybody working on this map. The more people that know about it, the more people will want a share of the treasure."

Tony said, "But Rosa is really smart in school. She's good at word games. And besides, three heads are better than two."

Salt said, "Well, all right. But three people it is, and no more. The three of us will work on the code. If we crack it, we share the treasure three ways. If we don't crack the code, we're out. Is that a fair deal?"

"That's a fair deal," Rosa said.

[1]

So they went up to the room with the captain's chest. They crowded around the table. Salt unfolded the map and laid it on the table. Then he held his glass in front of the map. "There it is," he said.

And there it was. There was an island in the middle of the map. The island was shaped like a thick letter *S*. And there were these numbers at the top of the map:

19—19—6—15—9—12
18—15—19 5 9—19—12—1—14—4

On the island were some letters, and there were more numbers. There were arrows joining the letters and numbers.

[1]

Old Salt said, "If only we could find out where this island is, we would be off to a good start. But there must be a thousand little islands in the South Pacific. This could be any one of them. Look for yourself."

Salt pointed to a big wall map of the South Pacific. It was dotted with little islands. Most of them looked like specks. You couldn't tell from the map if they were shaped like an *S*, like a *C*, or like an *I*. All of them looked like little dots.

Salt said, "I think those numbers at the top of the map tell where the island is. But I haven't been able to crack the code."

[2]

Rosa asked, "Could those numbers stand for compass readings?"

"Not a chance," Salt said. "That's the first thing I worked on. Those numbers make no sense in terms of a compass."

Rosa said, "This doesn't look too hard."

Salt said, "It must be hard or somebody would have cracked the code before."

Tony and the others worked on the code for an hour. Suddenly Tony said, "What if those numbers stand for letters?"

Salt looked up. Rosa stared at Tony a moment. Then Rosa said, "That's it. What if the number 1 stands for the letter *A*?"

Salt said, "And 2 would stand for *B*, and 3 would stand for *C*."

[1]

Rosa grabbed some paper. Here is what she wrote:

A	B	C	D	E	F	G	H	I
1	2	3	4	5	6	7	8	9
J	K	L	M	N	O	P	Q	R
10	11	12	13	14	15	16	17	18
S	T	U	V	W	X	Y	Z	
19	20	21	22	23	24	25	26	

Then Rosa looked at the numbers at the top of the map:

19—19—6—15—9—12
18—15—19 5 9—19—12—1—14—4

She said, "Let's see what we spell when we put the right letter for each of these numbers."

The first number was 19. So Rosa wrote *S* below that number. Rosa put in letters for each of the other numbers. Then she could see what it said at the top of the map.

[1]

1

A	B	C
chick	seal	fall
check	soil	fail

D	E	F
sprang	burn	sitting
sprung	barn	setting

2

poison   larger   beaches   sea

want   washes   worn   darted

paces   finger   thousands   watch

3

sprang   flowers   coral   volcano

roses   thorns   speck   solved   sense   bunch

magnifying   glasses   treasure   pointed

sure   waves   peered   able   island

4

The Code Is Broken

Tony and Rosa and Old Salt broke part of the map's code. The numbers on the top of the map said: "SS Foil, Rose Island."

"Rose Island," Old Salt said. He sprang from his chair and darted to the map. "It's right around here," he said. He pointed to three or four places on the map. Then he asked, "Where's my glass? How can I read this map without my glass?"

Rosa handed him the big magnifying glass. "Here it is," Salt said, and pointed to one of the little dots between two larger dots. "Rose Island," he said. "I remember it well. Flowers, trees, and black-sand beaches. The water is filled with poison coral. If you step on it, you're dead."

[1]

"Did you say the sand on the beach is black?" Rosa asked.

"As black as night," Old Salt said.

"I've never seen black sand," Tony said.

"You see," Salt said, "at one time—thousands and thousands of years ago—Rose Island was a volcano sticking out of the sea. The waves have worn the island down over the years. The rock from the volcano is black, so the sand on the beach is black."

"Wow!" Tony said. "Why do they call it Rose Island?"

"Because of the roses," Salt said. "Big roses, they are, with thorns as big as your finger."

[1]

Tony and the others stared at the speck on the map for a while. Then Salt went back to the table and sat down. "Give me my glass," he said.

Tony handed him the magnifying glass, and Salt held it near his eye and peered at the map.

"We've solved part of the code," Salt said. "But we still don't know what all these letters stand for. I'm sure that the letters tell us how to get to the treasure, but what do they mean?"

Rosa said, "There are some numbers on the map, too." Rosa pointed to the number 16. "This stands for *P.*"

"Yes," Salt said. "There are a lot of number 16's on this map. But what do they stand for?"

[2]

Rosa said, "Look. The number 16 is always next to a letter." Rosa pointed to a letter. Next to it was 16. Rosa pointed to another letter. Another 16 was next to this letter. Rosa said, "The number 16 is *P.* So these letters must have something to do with *P.* What's *P?*"

"Paces," Salt said and sprang from his chair again. "It's got to be paces."

Rosa looked at Tony. Tony looked at Rosa. The old man gripped the map and walked around the room looking at it. "Sure. Paces. And I think I know what the letters stand for on the map."

"What?" Rosa asked.

"The letters stand for numbers."

[2]

Rosa looked at Tony. Tony looked at Rosa. The old man dashed back to the table and sat down. "We can use the list that Rosa made out," he said. "The number 1 stands for the letter *A.* So the letter *A* must stand for the number 1."

"Sure," Tony said. "That makes sense."

"Let's see," Salt said. He pointed to Z—16.

"That means twenty-six paces."

During the next hour, they worked on the map. By the time the hour had passed, they had filled in all the letters and numbers on the map. Then Salt said, "Now we know how to get to that treasure."

On the next page is the map of Rose Island. See if you can find out how to get to the treasure.

[2]

19-19-6-15-9-12
18-15-19-5 9-19-12-1-14-4

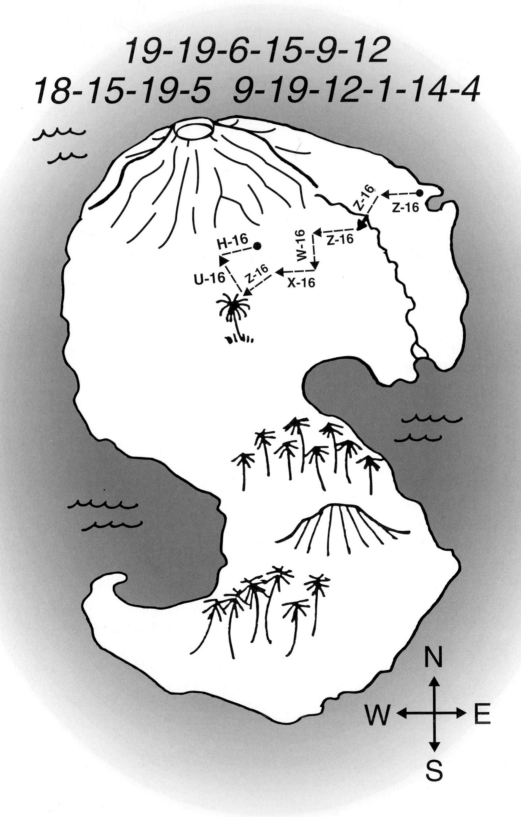

1

A	B
some	somebody
to	tonight
any	anybody

2

boiling   certain   sharply   face
straight   price   while   alarm
place   dream   load   chart

3

eight   weigh   child   knew   peered
gold   island   don't   woke   nobody
Rizzo   how   worth   cheek   asleep
gifts   already   tomorrow   adult   buy

Dreams of Gold

Now Tony and Rosa and Old Salt had broken the whole code. Numbers stood for letters, and letters stood for numbers. Z—16 was a code for twenty-six paces.

"Not a word of this to anybody," Old Salt said when Rosa and Tony were leaving his house. "Tonight we cracked the code. Tomorrow I'll see about getting on a ship to Rose Island."

Rosa and Tony walked slowly down the street. They talked for a while in front of their house. Then they went inside. Tony went to his bedroom and sat on his bed. He sat for a long time, thinking about the map and the treasure. It was funny, thinking about a real treasure.

[1]

Tony felt like an adult and a child at the same time. He felt like an adult because treasure-hunting is something that adults do. On the other hand, he felt like a child because he wanted to tell everybody about the treasure. He wanted to tell his mom and his dad, his little brother, and his dog. He wanted to tell his friends at school. He wanted to tell everybody.

Think of it—Tony Rizzo finding a treasure! Was all of this real, or was Tony just having a dream? Would he soon hear the buzz of an alarm clock going off for morning?

[1]

He shook his head and started thinking about gold. Gold. Gold was something that you read about in fairy tales. Gold was something for wedding rings. That was about the only place Tony had ever seen gold—real gold. He kept trying to think about how much money gold was worth. But he wasn't sure. How much does a chunk of gold weigh? How much gold would be in the chest? How much would the chest be worth?

Tony asked himself these questions. But he wasn't sure of the answers. So he began to think of something else.

[1]

He began thinking about how he would spend the money he got from the treasure. He'd buy the best bike in town. He'd get a motorcycle, too. Maybe he'd buy a motor boat. Maybe he'd buy two motor boats. Maybe he'd buy gifts for everybody. He could give his mother a new coat. He could give his father a new car. He could give his brother a horse. He could give himself five or six horses.

"Tony, are you up there?" It was his mother calling from downstairs.

"Yeah, it's me," he said. "I'm getting ready for bed."

"Well, it's late, Tony. You should be asleep by now."

[1]

So Tony went to sleep. And what do you think happened in his dream? Tony was trying to move a chest of gold. But it weighed so much that he couldn't make it move. That was pretty bad. And in Tony's dream, three people were after him. They were running to where the chest was. If he couldn't move the gold, they would take the chest. If he tried to stay with the gold, they would catch him. If he ran away, he wouldn't have the gold. So again and again, in his dream, he tried to move the chest. But he couldn't.

[1]

Tony woke up three or four times that night. In the morning he dressed quickly and left for school as soon as he had eaten. He stopped off at Old Salt's house and called, "Hey, Salt."

Salt came to the window. "What is it?" he barked.

"How much is gold worth?" Tony didn't mean to ask Salt about the price of gold. He really wanted to talk to Salt. He wanted to see the map and make sure that it wasn't part of his dream. He wanted to talk to somebody who knew about the treasure. But Tony didn't know how to tell this to Salt. If he had tried, it would have sounded silly.

[2]

"That's not a thing to be talking about," Salt said sharply. He looked boiling mad. "Don't talk about gold," he said.

"I'm sorry, Salt," Tony said. "Are you going to see about getting a ship?"

Salt shook his head. "Don't talk about that," he said. "Just go off to school and think about something else."

So Tony went to school. It seemed like a long day. It seemed as if the three o'clock bell would never ring. But at last it did, and Tony ran all the way to Salt's house. Now he would find out about the ship.

[1]

1

A	B	C
coil	smell	want
coal	small	wait

D	E	F
boiler	deck	paces
broiler	dock	places

2

tion   nation   station   vacation   location

3

parents   permission   thought   were
South   trapped   Pacific   upstairs
Wake   saying   thinking   Island   bite
trying   travel   you're   didn't   who
eight   weight   treasure   somebody

4

How to Get to Wake Island

Tony could hardly wait to get to Salt's house and meet with Salt and Rosa. There was a lot to talk about. All day in school Tony had thought about the treasure.

When Tony got to Salt's house, Rosa was already there. And Salt was boiling mad. Salt was saying, "You've got to stop talking about gold." Then his voice became soft. "Somebody will steal the map if you don't stop talking about it."

Tony said, "Well, I just can't stop thinking about it."

"Think all you want," Salt said. "But when you feel like talking about it, just bite your lip."

"Okay," Tony said.

[1]

Salt led them to the upstairs room. Then they sat around the table. Salt said, "From now on, we will write in code. If you want to know something, write it in code."

"That's a good idea," Rosa said. "If we do that, nobody will know what we're saying."

"Right," Salt said. "Now let me tell you what I found out about the ship."

Rosa and Tony bent over the table. Salt talked very softly. He told them that a vacation ship was leaving for the South Pacific in three weeks. Salt said that he could get a job on that ship. The ship would go as far as Wake Island. From that point, Salt would have to rent a small boat and travel 500 kilometers to Rose Island.

[1]

After Salt had told them his plan, Rosa yelled, "Wait a minute. We're going to be out of school in two weeks. We'll be out for summer vacation. So why don't we all go on the ship to Wake Island?"

"No, no," Salt said. "I'll go alone."

Tony asked, "How are you going to lift that chest from the hole? You're going to need help."

Old Salt said, "When I dig up that chest, I'll find some way to bring it back."

"That's not fair," Tony said. "And it's not very smart. That chest will weigh a lot. You're going to need us to help you."

[1]

Old Salt rubbed his chin. Then he said, "How are you going to pay for the trip to Wake Island? I don't have any cash."

"We could get jobs on the ship," Rosa said. "If you can get a job, why can't we get jobs?"

Salt rubbed his chin. Then he tapped the table with his finger. Rosa and Tony waited.

At last Salt said, "That might work. Yes, that just might work. We'll sure give it a try."

[1]

Tony grinned. He grabbed Salt's hand. "Thanks a lot," he said. "Wow, thanks. Now all I need to do is talk my mom and dad into letting me go."

"Me, too," Rosa said. "That's not going to be very easy."

So that's how things were when Rosa and Tony left Old Salt. They had to get permission to go on the trip. But they couldn't tell anybody about the treasure.

When Tony and Rosa got home, they went to their mother and father. "Can we go on a trip to the South Pacific?" Tony asked.

Their father was setting the table. He almost dropped a plate when Tony asked that question. "What did you say?" he asked.

Tony asked again. Then his mom said, "No, Tony. You may not go."

[1]

"Come on," he said. "Please let us go. Old Salt is going. It will be a lot of fun, and it won't cost any money. We will work on the ship. Think of all the things we would see."

Their parents looked at them. "No," they said.

For the next three days Tony and Rosa tried to talk their parents into letting them go. They tried to point out what a good thing the trip would be. They pointed out how much they would learn from such a trip. But after they made the best points they could, their mom and dad still said, "No. And please stop talking about that trip."

[1]

1

tion nation
vacation reflection

2

A	B
pass	passport
some	somehow
when	whenever
after	afternoon
out	outfit
flash	flashlight

3

coil waited twice thirty
clinkers clearing office
chance during distance
choice furnace season

4

sweat weather shovels
head eight weigh tools
thought happened wore
parents kitchen boiler
hired axes mate ma'am
pressed blazing grit grime
shower gales piling

5

On the Ship

Tony and Rosa tried and tried to make their mother and dad let them go on the trip to the South Pacific. Then it happened. Somehow Rosa and Tony talked their parents into it. Maybe they wore their parents down. Maybe their parents just got tired of saying, "No." But it happened.

Their mother talked to their father. They all talked to Old Salt. Salt told their parents that he would look out for Tony and Rosa. Their parents talked some more. Then, after a week of talking and talking, the kids' mother and father said, "Well, all right. You can go."

Tony jumped up in the air. He yelled. Rosa ran around the kitchen. Then Tony and Rosa kissed their mother and ran over to Salt's house.
[1]

And somehow the kids got jobs on the ship. Rosa got a job waiting on tables. Tony got a job in the boiler room. The man who hired them told Tony, "This is a hard job, and I don't know if you can do it. But I'll give you a chance."

Everything was set. Salt got the tools they would need to dig up the chest. He had a coil of thick rope. He had shovels and burlap bags and axes. He also had a flashlight. He said, "I think we have everything we'll need." They all got their passports and their shots. Those shots made Tony sick for two days.

[1]

Then everybody waited for the day the ship would leave for Wake Island. The ship would leave at three o'clock in the afternoon. But Salt and the others had to be on board at eight o'clock that morning.

It was a big ship, but very old. The first mate met Salt and the kids on the dock. He told them about the trip. He said, "Most of the people who go on this trip are on their vacation. Our job is to see that they have a good time."

[1]

The first mate told Salt and the kids how they had to talk to the people on board. "Always say, 'Yes, sir,' or 'Yes, ma'am,' " he said.

The first mate showed Tony the boiler room. The room was very big, and the furnace was bigger than any furnace Tony had ever seen.

The first mate said, "This is an old ship. It runs on coal. The coal is fed into this furnace. After the coal burns, it turns into big clinkers. Your job is to remove the clinkers from the furnace." The first mate showed Tony how to do that.

[1]

Then the first mate said, "I'm going to light the furnace now. In about an hour, the clinkers will start to form. That's when you start working. You'll work for four hours and rest for four hours. Then you'll work for four more hours."

The first mate pressed a button, and a fire started in the furnace. Chunks of coal began to fall into the furnace. Soon a bright fire was blazing in the furnace. Soon it was so hot in the boiler room that Tony felt faint.

The man who had hired Tony wasn't kidding when he said the work would be hard.

[1]

For four hours Tony fished clinkers from the furnace. He had a long, pointed rod. He rammed this rod into clinkers. Then he lifted them from the furnace.

After four hours had passed, a sailor came up to Tony and said, "Okay, you're off for four hours." Tony was a mess. He was covered with grit and grime. His face was streaked with sweat. His hands were sore. His legs were weak.

He walked to a corner of the boiler room and sat down. Before you could count to thirty, he was sound asleep.

[1]

Tony woke up about two hours later. He wouldn't have to start work again for two hours, so he took a shower. Then he changed into a clean outfit and went to see what Salt and Rosa were doing.

Salt's job was to talk to the people on board and answer their questions. When Tony found him, he was sitting in a deck chair talking to a man and a woman. He was telling them about the weather on Wake Island. Salt was saying, "During this season, the weather is fine. There are no gales." Salt had a pretty easy job.

Rosa was working in the dining room. When Tony saw her, she was clearing the dishes from a table and piling them on a tray. Her job looked pretty easy, too.

[2]

1

A	B	C
reach	dock	walk
reaches	docked	walking

D	E	F
rose	show	wave
roses	shown	waved

2

dead   sweat   weather   head

3

stout   flowers   speedboat
location   dealing   sharply
shouting   furnace

4

crawling   wild   child   lower
rent   scow   motor   craft
suckers   spare   interested
again   fifty   begin   deck   docked
taking   talking   eight   weigh

5

Wake Island

Salt, Tony, and Rosa had jobs on the big, old vacation ship, and it was going to the South Pacific. At first Tony was mad because his job was so hard. Rosa and Salt had easy jobs. But by the time the ship reached Wake Island, Tony was beginning to think that he had the best deal of the three. He toiled harder than the others, but his job made him very strong. His hands became strong from gripping that clinker rod. His back and legs were strong. When the ship docked at Wake Island, Tony was in the best shape he'd ever been in. [1]

The sun was boiling hot that day. Rosa, Tony, and Salt stood on the lower deck of the ship and looked at Wake Island. The ship's horn was going, "Toot, toot, toot." Other ships and small boats were tooting back. The people on deck were waving and shouting. The people on the dock were waving and shouting.

As Tony stood there, he could hardly believe what was happening. His home and his school seemed very far away. He had been on the ship for thirty-two days. [1]

The ship had made five stops. This was the last one. It would stay at Wake Island for three days. Then it would go back home. But Tony, Rosa, and Salt would not be on it. They would be in a small boat on their way to Rose Island.

That night Tony, Rosa, and Salt were standing on the dock again, talking to a woman who had small boats for rent. The night air was sweet with the smell of wild flowers. And the air was hot and wet.

Salt was saying to the woman at the dock, "We need a boat that can go one thousand kilometers out to sea."

[1]

"Where are you going?" the woman asked.

Salt slapped a bug on the back of his neck. Then he said, "We're going to look at some of the islands in the chain. We're interested in trees and other plants, we are."

"There are a lot of trees here on Wake Island," the woman said.

"No," Salt said sharply, "not the kinds of trees we're looking for. We have to go to the little islands."

The woman said, "There are a lot of little islands out there, all right."

Bugs were crawling all over Tony. He kept slapping them, but more bugs kept coming.

[1]

The dock woman said, "I think I have what you need." She pointed to an old scow. "That is a fine boat."

Salt shook his head. "What kind of fools do you take us for? We need a boat that is at least six meters long. It must have a good motor. And it must be a stout craft."

"That's a fine boat," the woman said. "But I have others. They cost a little more. I can give

you a good deal on that boat right there."

"Show us the others," Salt said. So the woman showed them three boats.

[1]

Salt didn't take the one Tony liked best. Tony liked a red-and-white speedboat. Salt picked a long, skinny boat. "How much?" he asked.

"For you," the woman said, and rubbed her head, "for you, I'll let you have it for—a hundred dollars a day."

Salt turned to Tony and Rosa. "Come on, kids," he said. "Let's get out of here. This woman thinks she's dealing with a pack of rich suckers."

Salt started to walk away. Then the woman called, "Wait. I'll let you have it for ninety dollars a day."

Salt turned around. He said, "We walk ten steps from you, and you dropped the price ten dollars. Why don't you wait until we walk fifty steps? Then we may be able to come to terms."

[2]

The woman looked shocked. She said, "Do you think that I would rent that boat for only fifty dollars a day?"

Salt said, "If you rent it to us, you rent it for fifty dollars a day."

It was much later when the woman finally gave in, but at last she said, "All right, you can have it for fifty dollars a day."

Salt said, "And with the tank filled with gas and with the spare tank filled with gas."

"All right, all right," the woman said.

Salt turned to Rosa and Tony. "We're all set. Sleep well tonight. When the sun comes up in the morning, we'll be on our way."

[1]

1

A	B	C
pile	gale	blaze
piling	gales	blazes

D	E	F
mate	hire	late
mates	hired	later

2

head   sweat   bread   weather

3

leave   starting   once   snored
protection   reflection   chain
smooth   bounced   starter
surface   distance
whenever   flashlight

4

claws   crawling   shovels
plowed   bobbing   swells
tomorrow   across   suddenly
bananas   speckled   dizzy
head   tiny   slid   plenty
volcano   chu-cug   gallons
steered   wild

5

The Trip to Rose Island

The sky in the east was starting to turn yellow. The sea was as smooth as a sheet of glass. Every now and then a little fish would pop out of the water and leave a ring that moved slowly and seemed to melt into the smooth surface of the water. The vacation ship was dark, except for a string of lights on the top deck. Little birds were walking on the beach. So were big crabs with claws that could cut off your finger. The bugs seemed to be everywhere. The boat was almost packed.

"Where are the shovels?" asked Rosa.

"They're packed," Salt said.

[1]

"What about food and water?" Tony asked.

"We <u>have</u> plenty," Salt said.

Rosa said, "That means we're ready to go."

Tony said, "What about gas?"

"We have plenty of that, too," Salt said.

Tony jumped into the boat. It didn't rock much, but it sent out three waves. The waves moved across the still water. Then Rosa got in the boat. And then Salt started the motor.

"Rrrrr-rrr-rrrr," went the starter. Then, "Chu-cug, chu-cug," went the motor. The boat started to move. The three of them were going out into the still sea, all alone.

[1]

The boat began to move faster. White water began to boil around the front of the boat as it plowed a path in the water. Behind the boat was a trail of V-shaped waves. Tony looked back at the dock. Everything was so quiet. The only sound was the "chu-cug, chu-cug" of the motor. Everything else was still.

That was in the early morning. By noon the sea had changed. Now the boat was bobbing over swells that were at least seven meters high. Up and down, and down and up.

Salt smiled and yelled, "This is the life. The sea—you can reach out and grab it. You can smell it. You can feel it in your bones!"

[1]

Rosa turned to Tony. "I feel sick," she said, but Tony didn't hear her. Tony was looking at a chain of tiny islands. Every time the boat reached the top of a green swell, Tony could see them off to one side. But when the boat slid down the back side of the swell, Tony couldn't see the islands any more. All he could see was water, water, water.

Salt pointed to the islands. "Yes," he said, "we'll see islands all the way to Rose Island, but we won't be there for some time."

[1]

"How much longer before we get there?" Rosa asked.

"Oh," Salt said, "if we don't come up against a big wind, we should be there by noon tomorrow."

"Oh, no," Rosa said.

Tony said, "Rosa, why don't you try to get some sleep? Maybe you'll feel better."

"No," Salt said. "If you feel sick, go to the front of the boat and look out across the sea as far as you can. Don't close your eyes."

So Rosa went to the front of the boat. She stayed there all day. When the sun was setting, the sea suddenly became still again. The stars came out. They seemed brighter than any stars Tony remembered.

[1]

Each star had a reflection in the water. The sea seemed to be speckled with stars.

Tony was dizzy. He had bounced up and down all day, and now he felt as if he were still bouncing.

Rosa said, "I'm hungry. When are we going to eat?"

"Eat?" Salt said. "Why, you can eat whenever you wish. And you can eat as much as you wish." He tossed a large cloth sack to Rosa. She opened the sack and looked into it. Then she reached inside.

[1]

"There are only bananas in this bag," she said.

"Bananas are good for you," Salt said. "Eat up."

Rosa said, "Is this all we have to eat?"

"That's all," Salt said. Nobody said much after that. Rosa picked out three bananas. Then she passed the sack to Tony. Tony ate five bananas. Then he drank three cups of water. He didn't feel hungry any more, but he sure didn't feel as if he'd had a good meal.

Then Tony leaned back and rested his head against the sleeping bags. He closed his eyes. The motor was going, "Chu-cug, chu-cug." The air was cool.

[1]

Suddenly somebody was shaking Tony. It was Salt. Tony must have fallen asleep. Salt was saying, "Come on, my lad. It's your turn to take the wheel."

Tony rubbed his eyes and sat up. Salt turned on a flashlight and handed him a compass. Salt pointed to a mark on the rim of the compass. "Keep the front of the boat pointing at this mark. This will take us straight to Rose Island."

So Tony took the wheel and steered the boat. Salt curled up in the back of the boat and went to sleep. He snored very loudly. Rosa was sleeping in the front of the boat. The air was cool now, and everything was quiet.

[1]

1

A	B	C	D	E
tape	soak	tire	whack	sweat
taped	soaking	tired	whacks	sweats

2

A	B
under	underbrush
land	landmark
after	afternoon

3

reflection   according   boil

protection   curl

4

machete   fortune   engine   rim

across   choppy   spray   bobbing

cliffs   cove   dizzy   speck

wobbly   shore   realized   tangle

calm   against   clear   volcano

5

Rose Island at Last

Tony steered the boat most of the night. When the sky began to grow light, the sea became choppy again. Each time the front of the boat went through a wave, water sprayed into the air. Some of it landed in the boat.

"Hey," Rosa said, "turn the boat so that it doesn't make so much spray."

Old Salt jumped up from the back of the boat. "You'd have Tony do that?" he yelled. "You'd have him miss Rose Island after we've come all this way?"

"No," Rosa said. "I'm just getting tired of getting wet."

[1]

Salt smiled. A wave with a curl of white water slapped the front of the boat. Rosa was soaked. Salt was soaked, but he kept on smiling. Then he said, "There she be. There be Rose Island."

Tony tried to stand up. But the boat was bobbing so much that it knocked Tony down.

"We're there," Salt said. "We'll be on dry land before you know it."

Two hours later, the boat was next to the island. They hadn't landed yet, but they were near the cove on the north end of the island. Tony watched the waves dash against the high cliffs of the island.

[1]

The island didn't look the way Tony had thought it would. It looked much bigger than he had thought. And the cliffs were much higher than he had thought.

At last, the boat came to a place where there were no cliffs. There was a little cove. The water in the cove was clear and very green. Tony could see fish swimming under the surface of the water. The boat slid up on the black-sand beach. Salt cut the engine, and everything was calm, except for the hooting of birds.

"All right," Salt said. "Grab the tools and let's be off to find our fortune of gold."

[1]

Tony grabbed two shovels and a coil of rope. When he began to walk across the beach, he realized that he was dizzy. It felt as if the beach were rolling this way and that way.

Rosa said, "Tony, you walk the way I feel. I'm dizzy."

Old Salt laughed. "You'll be a little wobbly for a few hours, but you'll get over it."

Tony followed Salt up a large hill. When they got to the top, Tony was out of wind. He looked back down the hill. The boat looked like a tiny speck on the shore of the cove.

[1]

"We've come a long way," Tony said.

"Not on the map, we haven't," Salt said. "We have gone up a lot, but we haven't gone very far from the shore." Salt took out the map. "We're at the rim of the hill now. So we can start pacing." He rubbed his chin. "According to the map," he said, "we should start pacing from a place that is a little north of the cove and east of the volcano. But I can't see the volcano. All I can see is a jungle."

Salt was right. To the west there was nothing but a tangle of green vines and trees. Beneath the trees were plants with leaves bigger than Tony.

[1]

"I'll have to climb a tree," Salt said. And he did. He found a tall tree near the rim of the hill. The tree had heavy vines growing around its trunk. Salt climbed all the way to the top. Then he locked his legs around the tree, took out his compass, and looked at it.

Salt yelled, "Go about a hundred meters north of here." Tony and Rosa ran north along the rim of the hill.

"That's good," Salt said.

[1]

Then Salt climbed back down the tree like a monkey. He ran up to them, pointed toward the jungle, and said, "We go that way twenty-six paces."

So they began to walk. Salt went first. He took out a large machete and whacked a path through the underbrush. The air felt wet in the jungle. And the plants spit out juice when Salt's machete cut through them. Tony was sweating. So were the others.

"Twenty-five . . . twenty-six," Salt said, and stopped. Then he turned to Rosa. "You stand on this spot. Tony and I will look for a landmark. If we can't find a landmark, we won't know if we are too far north or too far south."

[1]

Salt handed a machete to Tony. Salt said, "Cut a path south. Be careful of the plants. Some of them have thorns and sharp blades."

Tony went south. Salt went north. Tony had gone about ten meters when he came to a large rock. It was twice as tall as Tony, and it was covered with moss.

"I think I've found a landmark," Tony called.

Salt came running through the jungle. He smiled. The sweat was streaming down his face. He slapped the huge rock. "So you did, my boy. You found a real landmark. This is what we're looking for. It won't be long now before we reach the treasure."

[1]

1

A	B	C
ge	engine	ledge
gi	edge	huge
	bridge	change
	large	strange

2

excited   coil   filtered   fallen   curl   first

3

A	B
sun	sunlight
under	underbrush
south	southwest

4

ocean   knot   course   few   grew
machete   fortune   wild   white
world   trunk   dense   stream
lucky   jungle   arrows   squinted
beetle   rotting   twist   moment
full   tied   throw   sure   ferns

5 More Landmarks

Everything was green inside the jungle. Even the light was green. Tony's white shirt looked green. No sunlight got through the dense trees. Only a green glow filtered down to the floor of the jungle.

Salt was leading the way. Tony followed. Then came Rosa. After they reached the huge, moss-covered rock, they turned slightly to the south and paced off another twenty-six paces. They stopped at the edge of the stream. They jumped across the stream, turned more toward the west, and paced off another twenty-six paces. They stopped at the edge of a very steep slope.

[1]

"This must be the foot of the volcano," Salt said. "So far we've been lucky. There has been a landmark for every arrow on the map."

Now Salt and the others turned south. The map said W-16. So Salt stepped off twenty-three paces and stopped. There was no landmark.

Salt mopped the sweat from his face. He squinted and looked through the underbrush. "No landmark," he said. "But let's go on. We know that we were going right when we got to the foot of the volcano."

The next arrow on the map was pointing due west. The map said X-16. "Twenty-four paces," Salt said and began to step them off.

[1]

When Salt stopped, he looked around. Tony and Rosa looked around. No landmark. Salt shook his head. The jungle was not as dense as it had been. There were a few plants. Most of them were huge ferns. It would have been easy to see a landmark. But there was none.

"What should we do?" Tony asked.

Salt ran his sleeve across his face. "What should we do? Do you think that we came across the ocean so that we could stop here? We're going on. That's what we're going to do!"

Salt took out his compass, turned to the southwest, and checked the map. "Twenty-six paces," he said, and began to step them off.

[1]

When Salt stopped he shook his head. No landmark was in sight.

"This doesn't look good. We'll find that treasure, all right. But we may have gone off course back there."

With that, Salt sat down on the ground. The ground was almost bare. And it was wet, as Tony found out when he sat down.

Suddenly a big beetle, almost as big as your fist, darted across Tony's leg. Tony jumped up. "What was that?" he yelled. He could feel his heart pounding in his ears.

[1]

Salt laughed. "That, my boy, is what we call a bug. It's not a big bug for this part of the world, but it's a bug just the same. And we'll be living with lots of bugs for the next few days."

Tony almost said, "Let's go back. Let's forget about the gold and get out of here." But he knew that it would be silly to leave when they were so close to the treasure. So he didn't say anything.

Tony didn't want to sit on the ground any more. So he looked around for something else to sit on. He saw a fallen tree trunk a few feet from the others.

[1]

But when Tony walked over to the tree trunk, he didn't like the way it looked. It was rotting and falling apart. It looked as if it were full of all kinds of bugs. And it had a strange twist in the trunk. The trunk looked as if somebody had tied it into a knot.

A knot in the trunk of an old tree—it took Tony a moment to realize what that could mean.

"Hey," Tony yelled. "I found a landmark. Come here." The others ran over to the fallen tree. "Look at the trunk," Tony said.

[1]

"Sure," Salt said. "It's a mark all right. It was a young tree at the time they tied a knot in the trunk. The tree grew bigger and bigger. Then it died and fell over. In a few years there won't be anything left of it. But there it is, the landmark. We're right on course."

Tony walked to the roots of the old tree. He took out his compass and looked at the map. "U-sixteen," he said. "That means twenty-one paces."

Salt stepped them off. He stopped at the foot of a steep hill. Tony felt very excited. He knew the map by heart. He knew that there was one more arrow before the treasure— H-16.

[1]

Tony didn't wait for Salt. He began to pace off eight paces to the east. He stopped in front of a large pile of rocks.

"This is it," he hollered. "We found the treasure. It's under this pile of rocks."

He ran over and threw his arms around Rosa. Rosa was soaking wet. "We did it, Rosa," he said. "We're rich."

"Not yet, we're not," Salt said. "We're not rich until we get that treasure out of the ground."

Rosa said, "But we've already done the hard part. The rest is going to be easy."

"No, it won't," Salt said. "Our real work has just begun."

[1]

1

A	B	C
ge	huge	stranger
gi	engine	bridge
	change	germ

2

protection   clever   heaved   itched

crashing   uncoiled   crouched   chirping

selection   distance   vacation   cooler

3

pulled   rough   enough   hauled   knife

knot   moment   beginning

handle   minute   blade   allowed

flies   level   sunset   rattling

tackled   rumbling   distant   sore

rusty   tugged   realize   underbrush

bites   ocean   course   machete

Digging for Gold

Tony's hands were sore. His back was sore. So were his legs. He was beginning to realize that Salt had been right when he'd said that the real work was just beginning. For the past three hours, Tony had hauled rocks from the pile. At first the pile had been about two meters high. Now it was only about half a meter high.

Tony bent down and grabbed another rock. When he picked it up, he saw something below it. "Hey, Rosa," he said. "What's that?"

Rosa tossed a rock into the underbrush.

Then she wiped the sweat from her eyes. She bent down and looked where Tony was pointing. "It looks like a knife handle," Rosa said. "I'll pull it out."

[1]

Rosa was about to grab the handle when Salt tackled her. "No," Salt yelled. Salt and Rosa tumbled over the rock pile. Then Salt sat up and said, "Don't touch it. It may be a trap."

"What do you mean?" Rosa asked. Rosa was rubbing her arm.

Salt said, "If you had a treasure in the ground, would you leave it without some kind of protection?"

"I don't know," Rosa said.

[1]

"Well, the people who put this treasure in the ground wouldn't do that," Salt said. "They wouldn't want some stranger to come along and take their treasure. So they probably fixed a trap. If anybody pulls out that handle, the trap goes off. And the stranger won't have to worry about hauling the treasure home. The stranger will be dead."

"How does the trap work?" Tony asked.

"I don't know," Salt said. "Go get the rope and we'll find out."

Tony ran and got the coil of rope. He gave it to Salt. Salt uncoiled the rope and tied one end of it around the handle of the knife. Then Salt stepped back about twenty paces.

[1]

"Get back," he said. "When I pull this rope, there is no telling what will happen."

Tony and Rosa ran far back into the jungle. They crouched down behind a large tree. The tree was covered with bugs, but they didn't seem to care. They were watching Salt.

"Here it goes," Salt said. He tugged on the rope. Nothing happened. The knife didn't budge. He tugged again, and again, and again.

Suddenly the knife came out of the ground. And just as suddenly there was a rumbling sound up the side of the volcano. The sound was followed by a huge pile of rocks. Down they came. They landed right where Tony and Rosa had been standing.

[1]

Tony shook his head and brushed a big beetle from his arm. "Wow," he said. "And to think that I was standing there a minute ago."

Rosa called, "Is it all right to come out now?"

"Yes, yes," Salt said. "It's time to come out and haul some more rocks from the pile." The pile was now about two meters high again.

"How did they do that?" Tony asked.

"It was pretty clever," Salt said. He held up the knife handle. There was no blade attached to the handle. There was an old, rusty chain.

[1]

Salt said, "That chain led to a pile of rocks up the side of the volcano. When I pulled on the chain, I pulled the bottom rock out. That allowed the other rocks to fall down."

So Rosa and Tony went back to the rock pile and heaved rocks. They were almost finished when the forest began to grow dark. And when the forest began to grow dark, flies and other biting bugs came out. They came in clouds. It was hard for Tony to work. He spent most of his time slapping bugs. They bit through his shirt and his pants. Most of the bites itched. Some of them hurt.

[1]

"I can't take much more of this," Tony said.

"Neither can I," Salt said. "Let's go where the bugs don't like to go."

"Where's that?" Rosa asked.

"Up the volcano," Salt said. "There should be a good breeze up there, if we go high enough. And it should be cooler up there."

So Salt, Rosa, and Tony began to climb the volcano. Tony was tired. But he didn't mind climbing the volcano. He didn't mind anything that would get rid of those bugs.

[1]

At last Salt came to a level spot. The breeze was blowing. The air was cool. Off in the distance, Tony could see the sunset and the sea. It was rough, with huge white caps rolling against the cliffs.

Suddenly Tony began to shake. "I'm cold," he said.

Salt said, "Just lie down and close your eyes. In a few moments you'll feel fine. You'll feel real fine."

So Tony lay back and closed his eyes. He could hear the sound of the distant waves crashing against the cliffs of Rose Island. He could hear the breeze rattling leaves in the trees. He could hear the night birds chirping. He felt very, very tired. Very tired.

[1]

LESSON 54

1 knife   know   knock   knot   knew

2

A	B	C
ge	edge	range
gi	change	magic
	large	charge
	ledge	strange

---

3 wrong   couple   find   breakfast
bananas   yesterday   coffee   clever
rusty   swallows   shovels   enough
rough   hauled   found

---

4 pulled   bitter   digging   soil
thousands   chunks   corner   coin
morning   drank   clink   gone

5 Where Is the Treasure Chest?

When Tony woke up, he smelled smoke. He looked around. There was Salt cooking something over a fire. "What are we having for breakfast?" Tony asked.

"It's a fine breakfast you'll have," Salt said. "Bananas and coffee."

"Oh," Tony said. He wasn't very hungry for any more bananas. He could still taste the bananas he'd eaten yesterday and the day before. But bananas were better than nothing. So Tony ate three bananas and tried to drink some of the coffee Salt fixed. That coffee was so bitter that Tony couldn't drink more than a few swallows.

[1]

But there was one good thing about the coffee. After you drank some of it, you couldn't taste bananas any more. All you could taste was coffee. And you could taste coffee all morning.

The taste hadn't left Tony's mouth by the time they reached the foot of the volcano. It hadn't gone away when Tony and Rosa started to work on the pile of rocks again. It hadn't even gone away when it was time to stop for lunch and eat more bananas. By the early afternoon all of the rocks had been removed from the pile.

Salt pointed to the bare ground. "The place where the knife handle was is where we start digging."

[1]

Everybody dug. Every hour they stopped and rested. They drank water—lots of water. Then they picked up their shovels and dug. The ground was soft and full of bugs and worms. Rosa pulled out a worm that was over a meter long.

As they dug down, the soil turned different colors. At first it was black. After they had dug down about half a meter, it turned yellow. It stayed yellow for about a meter. Then it turned light gray. The light gray soil was harder than the other soil.

Tony was in the hole, digging through the light gray soil. The hole was so deep that Tony could hardly look over the top of it. Salt said, "Stop digging. We're in the wrong place."

"What?" Tony said, and he threw down his shovel. "What do you mean?"

[1]

Salt said, "The ones who hid this treasure were very clever. They put the trap here, but they didn't put the treasure here."

"How do you know?" Rosa asked. "Maybe we'll find it if we keep on digging."

"No, no," Salt said. "Look at the sides of your hole. You can see how the soil changes color. That soil has been there for thousands of years. If you threw dirt into a hole, it wouldn't form bands like that. There would be some black dirt at the bottom of the pile. And there would be gray dirt near the top. We're digging in the wrong place."

[1]

"Where is the right place?" Tony asked. "This is the place that is marked on the map."

"Maybe it is," Salt said. "And maybe this is the place where you find something that marks the treasure if you know what you're looking for."

"We found the knife handle," Rosa said. "That shows we're in the right place."

Salt said, "Maybe the knife handle tells us where to go. Let's follow the chain and see where it leads us."

[1]

Salt pulled on the rusty chain. Chunks of rust fell off as he pulled. He began to follow the chain up the side of the volcano. About eight meters above the place where the knife handle had been, Salt came to a ledge. He called down, "Here's where the rocks were piled. Throw me a shovel."

Tony tossed his shovel. It didn't go up high enough. Rosa tossed her shovel. Salt grabbed it and disappeared. They waited.

Then Salt came to the edge of the ledge. He was carrying a shovel full of dirt.

[1]

Salt said, "Look at this." He held up a big clump of gray soil. Then he held up a bit of yellow soil. He dumped the dirt over the ledge. Tony and Rosa bent over the dirt. There was black soil, and yellow soil, and gray soil.

"You found it," Rosa said.

"That I did," Salt said. He was sweating and smiling. "That I did."

Tony and Rosa scrambled up the side of the volcano. Tony remembered to bring his shovel. When they reached the ledge they saw Salt bent over.

Without looking up, Salt said, "They put the treasure under the rocks. I don't see any more traps. Let's dig down and see what we find."

[1]

Salt pushed the shovel into the ground. "Clink." He tossed the dirt aside. And there it was, the corner of a treasure chest.

Tony began to dig. Slowly the dirt was cleared from the chest. It was rusty and there were a couple of holes in it. Salt put his finger in one of the holes. Then he brought out a round coin. It looked like a black penny.

"What's that?" Rosa asked.

Salt said, "I'll show you what that is." He rubbed the coin on the leg of his pants. Then he held up the coin. It was shining like the sun. It was bright. IT WAS GOLD.

[1]

1

A	B	C	D
beard	charge	drank	tackle
board	change	drunk	tangle

2

know   knot   knife   knew

3

buried   shoulder   iron   reflection
distance   protection   uncovered   scoop
shiny   rough   sparkled   stacked   couple
handfuls   looped   crown   worth   pulled
enough   thought   calm   wrong
swung   drinking   burlap   weighs

Gold, Gold, Gold

Salt, Rosa, and Tony had found the chest that had been buried on Rose Island. Salt reached inside a hole in the chest and pulled out a gold coin.

The top of the chest was uncovered. A large, rusty lock hung from the chest lid. Salt took his shovel and swung it hard. He hit the lock. Bits of rust flew into the air. The lock swung back and forth. Again Salt swung at the lock, and again bits of rust flew in the air. On the third swing, the lock fell to the ground in two pieces.

[1]

Salt wedged the scoop of his shovel under the lid of the chest and pushed down. Slowly the lid began to move. Rosa and Tony grabbed the lid and pulled up. The lid opened. For a long moment, they stared into the chest. Nobody said a thing.

Tony looked into the chest, and he felt very strange. He could hear himself breathing. In the distance were sounds of jungle birds. His eyes were fixed on what he saw inside the chest. It didn't look the way he had thought it would.

[1]

Tony had thought that he would see heaps of shiny coins and gold crowns. He had thought he would see huge red gems that sparkled and gold drinking cups. But he saw heaps of black coins. Some of them were covered with green mold. Some of them had specks of white on them, but most of them were black.

There were three or four bugs in the chest, too. They scrambled down between the coins when the chest was opened.

"Tony and Rosa," Salt said softly, "we have found the SS *Foil's* treasure. And what a treasure it is!"

[1]

Salt was talking louder and faster. "Do you have any idea how much this treasure must be worth?" He picked up a large coin. "How much do you think this coin is worth?"

"Twenty dollars?" Tony asked.

"It's more like three hundred dollars," Salt said. "And we have hundreds and hundreds of these coins. We have thousands and thousands. We're rich. We're rich."

Salt threw his shovel into the air. Then he began to dance around the chest. He was sweating and singing, "We're rich, Rosa. We're rich, Tony."

Rosa joined in. So did Tony. The three of them danced around the chest until they were dizzy.

[1]

Tony sat down on the damp ground. Salt was breathing hard. He said, "Now comes the real job of getting the gold out of here."

"That chest doesn't look very big," Rosa said. "The three of us could probably carry it."

Salt laughed. Then he said, "Let me show you something."

He walked to the place where the rope and the other tools were stacked. He picked up a small burlap sack and walked back to the chest. Then he began to fill the sack. When it was full, he handed the sack to Rosa.

"Here," Salt said. "See how much a couple of handfuls of gold weigh."

[1]

When Rosa grabbed the sack she almost fell over. The sack seemed to pull her to the ground. "Wow," she said. "That sack must weigh twenty-five kilograms."

"Let me see," Tony said. He grabbed the sack. It was much smaller than the rocks he and Rosa had moved from the pile, but it seemed to weigh as much as most of them. "Wow," Tony said. "You're right. This stuff weighs more than iron."

Salt said, "Yes, gold is much heavier than iron. There aren't many things in this world that weigh as much as gold."

[1]

Rosa asked, "Well, how are we going to get the gold out of here?"

Salt said, "A little bit at a time. We'll just have to make a lot of trips back to the boat. We'll fill the burlap sacks we brought with us and carry them back to the boat. And we'd better get started right now."

Salt went back to the tool pile and came back with three burlap sacks. He said, "Now don't try to fill these sacks all the way, or we won't be able to carry them. Fill them about two-thirds of the way to the top."

[1]

Soon three sacks were filled. Then Salt cut three pieces of rope. Each piece was about three meters long. Then Salt took a piece of rope. He tied both ends around the neck of a sack. Then he looped the rope over one shoulder and around his waist.

Salt began to walk. The sack dragged along the ground. "Let's try it this way," Salt said. "I think we won't get as tired if we drag the bags instead of trying to carry them."

So Tony tied a piece of rope around a sack. So did Rosa. Then they all began to walk through the jungle, back to the boat.

[1]

1

A	B
for	forever
after	afternoon
sun	sunset

2

drenched   breathe   storm   burning

together   shore   hardly   wondered

age   clenched   squall   decided   boiler

3

shoes   figured   ton   dragging   million

probably   through   stones   jungle   rough

done   gem   pulled   rang   buried

charge   engine   iron   calm   pray   easier

spoon   beach   couple   sweat   believe

4

Loading the Boat

Rosa, Tony, and Salt were dragging bags of gold back to the boat. Dragging the sacks through the jungle was not easy. The sacks would drop into little holes. They would catch on the underbrush. At one time Tony thought that it would be easier to lift his sack and carry it. So he carried it for about seven meters. Then he decided that it would be much easier to drag the sack.

Soon Salt and the others were standing at the rim of the hill that led down to the shore. Salt tied the three pieces of rope together.

Then he began to let the sacks slide down the side of the hill.

[1]

Rosa and Tony scrambled down the hill and held onto the sacks. Then they carried the sacks to the boat.

Salt stood up and mopped the sweat from his face. "Look around for some pretty stones," he said. "We'll put them in the sacks. Then if anybody looks into any of the sacks, the person will see stones, not gold."

"Good idea," Rosa said.

So Rosa and Tony went rock hunting. They found some pretty red stones and some that had streaks of white and yellow in them. They opened the bags and dumped the stones in. Then they tied up the bags and dropped them in the front of the boat.

[1]

Salt said, "I think it will take about seven more trips to bring all of the gold down to the boat."

"Seven more trips," Rosa said. "Wow. That's going to be rough."

Rosa was right. By the time Tony had made three trips, his back was sore. His mouth was dry. And he was drenched with sweat. By the time Tony had made five trips, he could hardly walk. He was in better shape than Rosa. Rosa had to stop and rest every few steps.

"The air is so wet I can hardly breathe," she said.

[1]

The afternoon sun was beating down on the beach when Salt, Rosa, and Tony came down the hill with the last of the sacks. The sand was so hot that Tony could feel it burning through his shoes. Even Salt was tired. Tony had been thinking that Salt could work forever without stopping. But now he was bent over, dragging the sacks through the soft sand.

At last Tony came to the hard, wet sand near the water. He had only a few steps more to go. Tony filled his last sack with stones. For a moment Tony wondered if he would be able to lift his sack into the boat. He clenched his teeth, closed his eyes, and lifted as hard as he could.

[1]

Slowly Tony lifted the sack and let it fall on the other sacks in the nose of the boat. Then he helped Rosa lift her sack into the boat.

"Thanks," Rosa said.

Salt counted the sacks. "Twenty-four sacks," he said. "Twenty-four sacks."

"How much do you think each sack is worth?" Tony asked.

"I've got that all figured out. There are about a thousand coins in each sack. That means that each sack is probably worth three hundred thousand dollars."

Tony could feel his mouth fall open. The sound of Salt's voice rang in his ear. "Three hundred thousand dollars."

[1]

Salt said, "And we have twenty-four sacks, which means that our treasure is worth over seven million dollars."

Tony looked at Rosa. Rosa was grinning. Then Rosa hit herself on the head. "I can't believe it. We each have more than two million dollars. I can't believe it."

Salt said, "Yes, all we have to do is get that gold back and we'll be rich. Just begin to pray that the sea doesn't decide to take our treasure from us. The sea has done that before. A storm sank the ship that was carrying the treasure. Another storm could take the treasure from us."

[1]

"Don't talk that way," Tony said. "We've got the gold and we're going to get it home. Right, Rosa?"

"Right," Rosa said. "If we have to swim home with those sacks, we'll get them home. Right, Salt?"

Salt smiled. "Yes. We'll get it home if the sea wants us to take it home. And I hope that the sea does just that. But remember, our boat is going to ride low in the water. There will be nearly a ton of weight in the front of the boat. A good squall could send our treasure to the bottom of the ocean. Let's just hope that the sea is calm and that no squalls come up."

[2]

1 rather   hounding   choppy
protection   sloshing   bail
hoarse   budge   ignition

2 above   eddies   beginning   shore   shoes
mountains   agreed   measured   reflected
twice   throughout   foggy   muffled
travel   gusts   swung   bucket
steering   decide   waded   within
tiller   buried   chance   shoulder

On the Sea

The sun was setting and the bugs were beginning to come out when Rosa, Tony, and Salt pushed the boat away from the shore. All agreed that it would be better to start back that night than to wait until morning. If they waited until morning, they would have to sleep up on the mountain, far from the boat. If they tried to sleep near the boat they wouldn't get much sleep, with the bugs hounding them all night. So they agreed that it was best to start their trip back that night.

[1]

"Rrr-rrr-rrr," went the starter. "Chu-cug, chu-cug," went the engine. Salt was right. The boat was riding low in the water. Even though Salt had left most of the tools in the jungle, the weight of the gold in the front of the boat held the nose down.

Salt, Tony, and Rosa were near the back of the boat. Rosa put her arm over the side and measured the distance from the top of the boat to the water. It was only about half a meter. A good-sized wave would wash right into the boat.

[1]

But the sea was very calm and the stars were reflected in the water. Rosa said to herself, "Sea, stay calm. Don't get choppy. Just stay calm."

And the sea stayed calm throughout the night. Tony slept some but he kept waking up every time the boat seemed to make a funny move. The air was foggy the next morning, and the sea was still calm. The air seemed heavy and damp. When they talked, their voices sounded muffled. Tony yelled a couple of times just to hear his voice. His voice didn't seem to travel very far in the fog. [1]

Salt said, "There's a chance that the sea will be like this all day. But then there's a chance that a stiff wind will come up and blow the fog away at any time."

It wasn't long before they found out what the sea had in store for them. Within an hour, a stiff wind began to blow. At first there were gusts of wind that made eddies across the water. Then the wind began to blow hard and steady. Within a few moments, waves began to form on the ocean. The first waves were small and choppy. These waves soon began to roll into larger and larger waves. [1]

Before long, the waves were rolling and boiling and pounding into the side of the boat. The fog was lifting now, and Tony could see that the ocean was a mass of white, foaming waves. The boat was rocking from side to side as the waves pounded against it. The sound of the waves was very loud.

Salt said, "We're going to have to change course. Unless we head into the wind, we'll sink. Those waves will soon be coming over the side of the boat." [1]

Salt swung the boat around so that its nose was heading into the wind. Now the waves were crashing into the front of the boat and sending spray into the air. Tony looked at the bottom of the boat. Already there was water in the boat, sloshing around as the boat rode up and down over the waves.

Just then a huge wave hit the front of the boat. It didn't lift the front of the boat the way the other waves did. It came over the front of the boat like a curl of green glass. It seemed to leap inside the boat and—"crash." [1]

The bottom of the boat now had nearly half a meter of water in it. The water outside the boat was almost on the same level as the water inside the boat.

"We're going down," Rosa yelled above the roar of the waves. "We're sinking."

"Bail," Salt yelled in a hoarse voice. "Bail. Grab a bucket—use your hands—use anything. But bail. And don't stop."

Another wave crashed against the front of the boat, and added about three centimeters of water. "Bail," Salt yelled. "One more like that, and we're done for." [1]

Tony grabbed a pail and started to throw water from the boat as fast as he could. Rosa was throwing water out with her hands. Salt was using two coffee cans. He was steering the boat by holding his leg against the tiller.

"Bail faster," Salt yelled. "Here comes another big one."

The wave washed over the front of the boat and sloshed water around inside. Tony said to himself, "This is it. We're going down." But somehow the boat kept floating.

Then Salt stood up and waded to the front of the boat. He picked up a sack of gold.

"What are you doing?" Tony shouted.

"I'm going to save us and the boat," Salt yelled. [1]

A	B
motor	motorcycle
through	throughout
out	outside

pail   tiller   surface   stretched   shine
chirp   centimeters   engine   force

pour   knot   hollered   above
moment   sore   seven   suddenly
dry   allowing   rolling   million
worried   afternoon   engine   few
sailor   trouble   minute   hungry
knew   calm   imagine   steering

Never Make Light of the Sea

Salt was in the front of the boat. He had just picked up a bag of gold and had told Tony that he was going to do something to save the boat. Salt threw the sack of gold. But he didn't throw it into the ocean. He threw it to the middle of the boat. Then he threw another bag, and another, and another. After he had moved more than ten of the bags, he came back to the tiller.

He hollered, "This will put more weight in the back of the boat. The front will be higher in the water. Maybe the waves won't come over it now."

[1]

Tony was still bailing. It didn't seem to be doing much to get rid of the water in the bottom of the boat. For every bucketful he removed from the boat, a wave added a bucketful. It went on that way for about an hour.

The back of the boat was only a little bit above the water. Every now and then it would sink below the surface of the water for a moment, and water would pour in over the back. Every now and then a huge wave would break against the front of the boat and send water flying into the boat.

[1]

The boat was climbing up one side of the waves and sliding back down the other. At times it seemed to Tony as if the boat was going straight up into the air, and then straight down. It was that way for an hour.

And then the wind began to die. When the wind stopped, the waves seemed to lose some of their life. They became more rounded. They didn't seem to fight as hard when they struck the boat. They didn't seem to jar the boat with the force they had when the wind was blowing. They didn't seem to move as fast.

[1]

Tony and the others were still bailing. They bailed until there were just a few centimeters of water in the bottom of the boat. Then Rosa said, "Let's stop."

"Let's not," Tony said. "We need a big head start on the waves if they're going to start kicking up again. Let's get every drop of water out of this boat."

And they did. When they finally stopped bailing, the bottom of the boat was almost dry.

Tony sat up straight. His back was sore. He stretched and looked up. The sun was out now. The air was hot and wet.

[1]

Salt smiled and began to sing, " 'Tis a sailor's life for me, for me. I sail the seven seas. I go where I go, because I know, this is the life for me."

Suddenly he stopped singing and bent forward. "I hope you will remember this. Never make light of the sea. The sea could have had our boat if it wanted to take the boat. It could have taken us if it wanted us. When you pass over the sea, remember that the sea is allowing you to pass."

[1]

Everyone was quiet for a long time. The only sound was the "chu-cug, chu-cug" of the engine. From time to time Tony looked at the waves. They were still pretty big, but the boat was rolling over them without any trouble.

Tony lay back and closed his eyes. He began to think about the gold. Imagine having two million dollars—two million dollars! What could you buy with all that money? You could buy a motorcycle—five motorcycles. You could buy a boat—any kind of boat you wanted. You could even buy a nice home for your family. You could buy anything you wanted. Wow!

[1]

Tony liked to think about these things. But every time he began to feel good about the gold, he remembered what Salt had said and became a little worried about the sea. Salt had said that they wouldn't reach Wake Island until just before morning. They would still be in the boat all afternoon, all evening, and almost all of the night. That was a lot of time. And the sea could change very quickly.

Tony opened his eyes and looked around. Rosa was eating a banana. The sun was very hot.

[1]

The rest of the day passed very slowly. Each minute seemed like an hour to Tony. Each hour seemed like a day.

"Come on," Tony said to himself, "we've got to make it."

Time moved slowly until about four o'clock in the afternoon. When it happened, Tony was trying to make up his mind about whether he was hungry enough to eat another banana. He had just about decided that he would eat one more—just one more—when the engine went, "Chu-cug, chu—" It wheezed a little, and stopped.

[1]

1

A	B
some	somewhere
through	throughout
any	anyone

2

touch   magneto   metal   cover   system

drifted   course   watching   squinted

listening   cocked   tense   darkness

dead   white   wheel   whispered   enough

appeared   transferred   pour

engine   ignition   imagine   edge   price

The Long Night

The engine had died. Tony and the others were somewhere in the South Pacific Ocean. They were more than a hundred kilometers from Wake Island. The sea was still rough. The boat was turning sideways and rocking as the waves struck it from the side.

"What's wrong?" Tony asked.

"I won't know until I look at the engine." Salt removed the metal cover from the engine. The engine looked small and old. Salt bent over it. He grabbed the spark plug. "Hit the starter," he said to Rosa.

"Rrr, rrr, rrr."

"That's enough," Salt said. "The engine is not getting a spark. Something's wrong with the ignition system."

[1]

Salt took out his knife and touched different parts of the engine. Then he shook his head. "The magneto is wet," he said.

"What do we do now?" Tony asked.

"Wait," Salt said. "The sun is bright and hot. With the cover off the engine, it should dry out in a little while."

Salt tried the starter every fifteen minutes. The third time he tried it, the engine started.

"Good deal," Tony yelled. "We're on our way again."

"Yes, we are," Salt said, but he shook his head.

"What's wrong?" Tony asked.

"We drifted quite a bit while the engine was dead," Salt said. "I just hope we didn't drift too far off course."

[1]

Tony didn't sleep that night. Neither did the others. Salt remained at the tiller. Rosa was sitting in the front of the boat now. Tony was in the middle. He was watching Salt's face. The moon was bright, and Tony could see Salt clearly.

Tony was watching Salt because Salt seemed to know what was happening. When he squinted and looked off to the east, Tony looked to the east. When Salt cocked his head and seemed to be listening to the sound of the engine, Tony cocked his head and listened. It went on like that throughout most of the night.

[1]

Morning was near now. This was the time they were supposed to reach Wake Island. Salt's face was tense. His head moved quickly—looking this way and that way.

"We should be seeing lights any time," Salt said. But no lights appeared. Salt looked up at the stars. Then he checked his compass. Then he began to look this way and that way again.

"I think I see something," Rosa said from the front of the boat. "Over there." She pointed to the west.

[1]

Tony squinted and looked where Rosa was pointing. He looked as hard as his eyes could look, but he didn't see anything.

"It's not there now," Rosa said. "But I saw a light over there."

The boat moved through the water, and everybody in the boat peered into the darkness. For an instant Tony thought he saw some lights, but then he realized that he was looking at the reflection of a star.

Suddenly Salt stood up in the boat. Then he stood on the seat. Then he said, "Wake Island is dead ahead. We'll be there pretty soon."

Tony grinned. "Good deal," he yelled. Everybody began to sing and laugh.

[1]

It seemed like a long time—a long, long time. But, at last, the boat was pulling up to the dock.

Salt leaned forward. "Remember," he said, "not one word about gold. We have sacks of rocks. Remember that."

Salt tied the boat to the dock. Then he whispered, "You stay here. I'll get a truck for the gold."

Tony and Rosa waited in the boat. Two women came down to the docks and went off in a white boat to fish. A gray dog came near, but when Rosa called, it ran to the other end of the dock and then disappeared.

[1]

At last Salt returned. He was driving an old truck. It looked like an old mail truck. It had a big sign in the rear window. "For Rent," the sign said. Salt parked the truck next to the boat. Then he, Rosa, and Tony transferred the gold from the boat to the truck.

After the truck was loaded, Salt drove the truck and followed a dirt road up a hill near the dock. There were no houses on the hill. Salt pulled off the road and turned off the engine. "We'll sleep here for a while, then we'll see about going home."

Tony and Rosa stretched out on the sacks of gold in the back of the truck. Salt went to sleep behind the wheel.

[2]

1

A	B
motor	motorboat
over	overlooking
air	airport

2

squall   third   night
loaded   parked   blushing
claim   section

3

insurance   Los Angeles   zone
ticket   Higgins   officer
customs   statements   true
discovered   fifty   pilot's
fellows   pictures   entire
well-wisher   welcome   shake
bald   delivered   banners
reporters   should   people

4

The Trip Home

Tony and the others slept in the truck. When Tony woke up, the truck was moving. Salt was driving the truck and singing, " 'Tis a sailor's life for me, for me. For I sail the seven seas—"

"Where are we going now?" Rosa asked.

"To the airport, Rosa, to the airport."

Salt parked in front of the airport in a no-parking zone. Then he got out of the truck.

"If a cop comes over here," Salt said, "tell him I'll punch him in the nose if he tries to give us a ticket."

[1]

"Do you really want us to tell him that?" Rosa asked.

"I sure do," Salt said. "Tell it like you mean it. I'll feel a lot better with a cop standing next to this truck."

Salt went into the airport. Just then a police car pulled up next to the truck.

"Move that truck," the cop said.

"We can't," Tony said. "We don't have the keys. But the man who is driving this truck said that he'd punch you in the nose if you gave us a ticket."

"He said that, did he?" the cop said. He got out of his car and walked to the front of the truck.

[1]

The cop made out a ticket and handed it to Rosa. Then he stood next to the truck and waited. In a few minutes Salt came out of the airport. He was walking with a tall woman.

"Hand out one of those bags," Salt said. "Mrs. Higgins wants to see the kind of rocks we found on Rose Island."

Tony slid one of the sacks along the floor of the truck. Salt grabbed it.

He untied it and tossed out the rocks. Mrs. Higgins' eyes seemed to pop out when she looked inside the sack.

"Yes," Salt said, "we've got twenty-four sacks like that one."

[1]

"What's going on here?" the cop demanded.

Mrs. Higgins said, "I think it's all right, officer. These people have found the *Foil* treasure."

"They did what?" the cop asked.

Mrs. Higgins pulled a handful of gold coins from the sack and showed them to the cop. The cop's eyes seemed to pop. "Are those gold coins?" he asked.

"Thousands and thousands of them," Salt said.

Salt, Tony, and Rosa spent most of the day filling out papers and talking to people. They filled out papers for insurance. They filled out papers to claim the gold. They talked to people from the newspapers. And they talked to Mrs. Higgins.

[1]

Mrs. Higgins was a customs officer. She wrote out the entire story of how Salt, Tony, and Rosa had discovered the gold. Then Salt, Rosa, and Tony filled out statements saying that the report was true. Mrs. Higgins told them that the gold would be delivered to a bank in their home town.

That night Salt, Tony, and Rosa stayed in a fine hotel overlooking the beach on Wake Island. Tony slept like a log. In the morning he ate eggs, and toast, and lots of juice. But he didn't eat one banana.

[1]

Later, a big black car took them to the airport. They were to fly back on a jumbo jet.

They sat in the first-class section of the plane. After the plane was in the air, the pilot's voice came over the loudspeaker. "We are glad to have three very happy people with us today. These people have done something that many others have tried to do over the last fifty years. They found the *Foil* treasure. The word that I have is that the treasure is worth about seven million dollars."

[1]

The people in the plane went, "Ooo," and "Ahhh," and "Wow!" Some of them clapped. Tony felt himself blushing.

The flight back home didn't seem to take much time. Tony remembered the days he had worked in the boiler room on the ship that went to Wake Island. The jumbo jet made it across the ocean in less than 12 hours.

Reporters met the plane when it landed in Los Angeles. They asked many questions and they took pictures. They invited Salt, Rosa, and Tony to have lunch with them.

[1]

The next day the three arrived home. Again they were met by reporters, and questions, and pictures, and invitations for lunch and dinner. People were waving and yelling. They were holding up banners that said, "Welcome home, Tony and Rosa."

There were no banners to welcome Salt home. But the reporters seemed to like to talk to Salt. They asked him most of the questions.

Then the last question had been asked, the last handshake was over, the last well-wisher had left. Tony, Rosa, their mom and dad went home. Their mom cried a little bit, but they could see that she was very happy and very proud.

[1]

1

A	B
news	newspaper
under	understand
gentle	gentleman
in	indeed

2

graduated   accounts   sixteen   tossed
stole   eight   blinked   interested
figuring   lonely   adventure   tomorrow
forward   world   friends   ashamed
barked   watch   invitation   insurance
range   police   officer

Salt's Real Treasure

The day after Salt and the others came home, Tony was reading accounts of the treasure hunt in the newspaper. One account said that they came back with sixteen bags of gold.

"That's not right," Tony said.

He glanced through another account. It said the same thing. It said that Salt and Tony and Rosa had found twenty-four sacks but brought back only sixteen.

The account said, "When Salt was asked what happened to the other sacks, he said, 'They went back to the sea.' "

Tony tossed the newspaper aside. He got Rosa and they ran from the house. They ran all the way to Salt's house. Salt was sitting on the front steps talking to three people.

[1]

Tony said, "Salt, can we go inside? We want to ask you something."

"Sure," Salt said.

So Tony, Rosa, and Salt went inside. They went upstairs to Salt's room. It seemed to Tony that it was a hundred years ago when they had been in that room before, looking at the map, trying to figure out how to crack the code.

Tony asked, "How many bags did we bring back?"

"I can see it in your face," Salt said. "You're thinking that Old Salt stole some of your gold. No, my boy, you have your eight bags and Rosa has her eight bags."

[1]

Tony asked again, "How many bags did we bring back?"

"Twenty-four bags," Salt said.

Rosa said, "But the newspaper said we brought back only sixteen bags. Where are your eight bags?"

"Where they should be," Salt said.

Tony looked at Rosa and blinked. Salt walked over to the desk picture of his captain. "Who led us to the gold?"

Rosa pointed to the picture. "I guess he did," Rosa said.

"Indeed he did," Salt said. "He sent us the trunk. And that trunk is what got you interested. Then he gave us the map. And then maybe he even gave us a little help in figuring out how to break the code."

[1]

Tony said, "But he's dead. You can't pay him back."

"Oh, can't I?" Salt said, and laughed. "My captain spent his last days in a home for old sailors. The days of an old sailor can be lonely, or they can be like a golden sunset. I think that my captain would want me to do something for that sailors' home. After all, the map came from the sailors' home."

Rosa asked, "Did you give all your treasure to that sailors' home?"

"No, Rosa," Salt said. "I didn't give them any of my treasure. I gave them nothing but gold. Eight tired little bags of gold. I kept the treasure for myself."

[1]

"What are you talking about?" Tony asked. "You gave them the gold—that's the treasure."

"No, no," Salt said. "The treasure was the adventure. You can't understand this because you're young, and you have your life in front of you. But for me, there were no plans. Tomorrow wasn't a thing I looked forward to. It was something I knew would come, and I knew it would be like the day before."

"But then I found the treasure of them all. I had a chance to be young again. Like a fool, I could make plans and dream of gold. I had two friends, and together we would go halfway around the world. That was the treasure. The gold was the reason, but the real treasure was you and Rosa, and the days we spent together."

[2]

Both Rosa and Tony looked at Old Salt. Tony felt very sad and ashamed. He said, "I see what you mean. We had some time, didn't we? I guess I'll remember that trip for the rest of my life."

"Me, too," Rosa said. "But what are you going to do for money, Salt?"

Salt stood up and waved his arms around. "I have this house. And how much money does an old man need? I suppose I'll spend most of my time sitting on the porch. Maybe I'll take a little trip once in a while. But I don't need much money. Besides, the sailors' home can make better use of that gold than I can."

Rosa said, "Do you think Tony and I should give some of our gold away?"

"No," Salt barked. "That gold is yours. You keep it and make good use of it. Just don't let it change your life. Remember, the gold is not the real treasure. The real treasure is the treasure hunt. The treasure is doing things and having good friends with you."

[1]

Tony remembered what Salt said. He remembered it for years, and he tried to follow the advice that Salt had given him. Tony didn't buy a lot of motorcycles and cars. He didn't act as if he were a big-timer. He and Rosa helped their mother and father buy a new house. Tony went back to school, and he worked hard. After he graduated, he went on to college and worked hard. Whenever he had a chance, he went to visit Old Salt. And once each year during the summer, Tony, Rosa, and Old Salt got together and talked about their adventure.

One more thing happened. After that adventure, nobody made fun of Old Salt.

[1]

1

A	B
drive	driveway
over	overlooking
birth	birthday

2

trout gear loaded partner sailors

entertainment sneakiest treatment

ostrich whoop dirty

reformed surprise whale

3

received New Bedford kilometers

Emma bluff Charlie assistant

banged event improve howled

ahoy laughter graduated

4

A Surprise Party

It was Salt's birthday, so Rosa and Tony decided to throw a big party at the old sailors' home. Rosa and Tony wanted to surprise Salt, so they didn't tell him about the party. But they tried to invite all of the people that he had talked about.

He had once talked about a rancher named Emma Branch, so they invited her. One time Salt had told a tale about a funny con man, so they invited him. And of course they invited all of the old people who lived in the home—men and women who had spent their lives sailing and fishing.

[1]

On the day of the party, Rosa and Tony went over to Salt's home. They pulled up in Rosa's car. "Salt," they called, "let's go for a little outing."

Salt said, "I'm ready for an outing. I thought I would go down to the stream and see if I could catch some trout."

"We wanted to go for a drive," Rosa said. "But why don't you bring your fishing gear along? We may find a place to do some fishing."

So Old Salt loaded his gear into the car, and the car took off down the street.

[1]

It was nearly a hundred kilometers to the old sailors' home. When Salt, Rosa, and Tony had gone over sixty kilometers, Salt said, "Where are we going?"

"We thought we'd stop off at New Bedford," Tony said.

"That's where the sailors' home is," Salt said. "Could we stop by there to say hello?"

"Sure," Rosa said. She and Tony smiled.

Salt directed them to the sailors' home. It was on a large bluff overlooking the sea. It was a big place with lots of rooms. Rosa parked the car in the driveway in front of the white house.

[1]

Salt got out of the car and stretched. Then he yelled, "Ahoy, there. Is anybody home?"

Nobody answered. Salt said, "Those folks must be hard of hearing. Let's go in and wake them up."

Salt, Rosa, and Tony went up the front steps and inside the building. It was dark in the huge living room. And it was very quiet.

"Where is everybody?" Salt barked.

Just then somebody snapped on the lights. Somebody opened the drapes. And everybody yelled, "Surprise! Surprise!"

Old sailors jumped up from behind couches and chairs. They popped out from behind the drapes and from behind the doors. They walked across the floor, yelling and laughing and slapping Salt on the back.

[1]

"You're a sight for sore eyes," the old sailors said to Salt.

For a few moments Salt stood there with his mouth open and his eyes wide. Then he began to yell and whoop it up.

"Charlie!" he yelled, and hugged one of the old sailors. "You old bum," Salt said, "I thought we saw you for the last time in South America."

Charlie tried to tell Salt how he got out of South America after the ship had sailed without him. But Salt couldn't hear what Charlie was saying. Other people were grabbing Salt, slapping him, jumping up and down, and having a whale of a time.

[1]

The rancher came out of the crowd. She picked Salt up and swung him around. "Good seeing you, you dirty old goat," Emma said.

"Put me down," Salt yelled. So the rancher dropped him on his seat in the middle of the floor. He shook his fist, and his face turned red. All the old people and the rancher howled with laughter.

Just then a man walked in the room. He was leading another man. He stopped in the middle of the floor. He said, "I am in charge of the entertainment. My assistant and I have lots of fun and games planned for everybody."

Old Salt said, "I don't know that fellow who's talking, but I know his assistant. He's the sneakiest sneak in the South Pacific—the con man himself."

[1]

The con man took a bow. The other man, the president, said, "I'll have you know that my assistant is a reformed man. He has received treatment at the Happy Hollow Rest Home. Isn't that right, corporal?"

"Yes," the con man said.

Everybody clapped. Some of the old people banged their canes on the floor.

"Our first event," the president said, "will be an egg-throwing contest. The rules are simple. You pick a partner. You stand two steps from your partner. You throw the egg. If your partner catches it without breaking it, each of you takes one big step backward. This keeps up until we have a winner."

"What happens if we break an egg?" one old woman asked.

"We pick you up and throw you off the dock," the president said. "But if you and your partner win, we have a fine prize for you. Everybody, go outside, and we'll line up for the game."

[2]

1

A	B	C	D	E
throw	woman	stream	drive	anybody
threw	women	scream	drove	nobody

2

rancher   loaded   partners   stream

catch   hearing   couches   bunch

leading   entertainment   sneakiest

3

caught   argue   arguing   pairs

silence   basket   ostrich   folks

splat   lousy   heave-ho   shaking

ladies   gentlemen   pie-eating

surrounded   battling   rooms

4

The Egg-Throwing Contest

Salt, Rosa, the rancher, and everybody else ran outside. Salt and Emma Branch were partners. Rosa and Tony were partners. All of the old sailors paired off. Some of them were laughing and horsing around.

"Silence," the president said. "We must have silence."

Everybody became quiet and looked at the president. Next to him was a huge basket.

"To make the game more interesting, we have large eggs," the president said.

Salt said, "Those are ostrich eggs. They are bigger than baseballs."

The con man passed out the eggs. The old folks laughed and talked with each other.

"Silence," the president said. "Everybody, line up and begin the game. Throw your eggs."

[1]

There were about thirty pairs of people playing the game. The eggs went into the air. Everybody caught the eggs except one man named Stan. His egg landed on his shirt with a "splat." Everybody but that man and his partner laughed.

Stan, the man who missed the egg, was madder than someone covered with cotton-taffy pike. He said to his partner, "Pete, you didn't have to throw a line drive at me."

"Line drive, my foot," Pete said. "If you had put your glasses on, you might have caught that egg."

"Pete," Stan said, "that was a lousy toss."

[1]

The partners kept arguing. Even as the con man and the president picked them up and gave them the heave-ho into the water, they kept arguing.

The game went on. Everybody took one more step back.

"Everybody, throw your eggs." Everybody caught the eggs.

"Take one big step back," the president said. "Throw your eggs."

This time two people missed. Both of them blamed the ones who threw the eggs. "Don't throw me in the water," one old man said. "It was that bum. He couldn't hit the side of a barn if he was locked inside."

"Splash!" Off the end of the dock the partners went.

[1]

The game went on. Soon there were only four pairs of partners left in the game. They were surrounded by people who were dripping wet and yelling and shouting, "Come on, toss those eggs," and "You're going to miss your egg."

When the partners were twenty steps apart, Tony missed his egg. Rosa threw it short and Tony made a diving catch. But when he hit the ground—"Splat"—ostrich egg went all over the place.

The others picked him up and threw him off the end of the dock. Then they threw Rosa in, too.

Now there were three pairs left. Emma Branch and Old Salt were still in the contest.

[1]

"Come on, Salt," the rancher said. "We can beat the rest of these bums."

The people began to yell, "No rancher can beat a sailor. Come on, beat that rancher."

The eggs went into the air. Emma caught the egg thrown by Salt, but—"Splat!"—it broke. Within two seconds, everyone grabbed the rancher and Salt.

"Splash! Splash!" They went into the water.

"Somebody's going to pay for this," the rancher said. She was sitting in the water, shaking her fist. One old man laughed so hard that he fell off the end of the dock.

[1]

One woman pushed a man off the dock. Then another man pushed Rosa. Then Tony pushed that man. Within a few moments, everyone was in the water.

"Stop this horsing around," the president shouted. "The game is not over yet."

Two pairs of old sailors were battling it out for the prize. They tossed the eggs. One old man missed. He jumped up and down and started to shout. But before he could say twenty words, he and his partner were in the water.

At last there was a winning team. Each old sailor on the winning team received a live, full-sized ostrich.

[1]

"Our next event," said the president, "will be a pie-eating contest. For this event we have set up a long table on the other side of the house, if you will follow me, ladies and gentlemen."

Everybody went to the other side of the house. The president pointed to a banana cream pie. "Now you must remember that this is a pie-eating contest. Let me go over the rules with you."

The president snapped his fingers, and the con man ran up to him. The president said, "In a pie-eating contest, you may not do this." He picked up the pie and heaved it into the con man's face.

"Splat!" the con man's face looked like a big puff of whipped cream.

[1]

"Also," the president said, "You may not do this." The president placed a pie on the table in front of the con man. Then he grabbed the con man by the back of the neck and pushed his face into the pie.

"That is against the rules," the president said.

Salt picked up a pie. He said, "Is this fair?" He tossed the pie and hit the rancher right in the face. "Splat!"

"No," the president said. "That is not fair."

Suddenly many pies were flying through the air. The president jumped up on the table. "We must have silence," he said. "We must have—"

"Splat!" Two pies hit him at the same time. Then many sticky hands grabbed him, lifted him from the table, carried him to the end of the dock, and—"Splash!"

[1]

1

A   B

tooth   toothpick
night   nightmare
birth   birthday

2

pie-eating splash cheered heap
worth sneak pairs around dreams
lousy person giant

3

brought flying sore laughing
glub finished glump sticky
chump turkey dragged hollered
clothes treasure ticket
twelve shoes belt feeding

4

The Sale

Salt was having a surprise party. Pies were flying, people were being tossed into the water, and everybody was getting sore sides from laughing so hard.

The old people had tossed the president into the water. "Please," the president said, "we must have a little order."

The president went back to the table and again explained the rules of the pie-eating contest. The con man brought out another load of pies, and the contest began.

"Glub, glump, chump, chump." Everybody ate pie and more pie. Pretty soon a very fat man said, "That's all. I'm finished. I hate pie." Everybody laughed.

[1]

The president spotted one person feeding pie to a dog under the table. A woman was trying to feed her pie to an ostrich, but the ostrich didn't like the pie. The ostrich liked a button on the woman's coat.

"Get out of here, you giant turkey," the woman yelled.

The winner of the pie-eating contest was a tall, slim man named Thin Jim. After everybody else quit, Thin Jim was still putting pie away. "I'm just getting down to my all-day pace. I could eat like this for days. I can eat more than anyone in these parts. I can eat more than—"

"Splat!" Three pies hit him at the same time.

[1]

Then many sticky hands picked up Thin Jim and pulled him from the table. They dragged him across the grass. They got him to the dock. "Splash!"

When Jim came out of the water he said, "You are just mad because I won the pie-eating contest."

"So you did," the president said. "And here is the first prize, a gold toothpick."

Everybody cheered and clapped as the president handed the prize to Thin Jim. Jim held up the toothpick so that all could see it.

"Silence, silence," the president hollered.

[1]

The president said, "Our next event is the sale. For this event, you have to bid for things I place on the block. Everybody has three chips. But if you want to bet more than three chips, you can bet your clothes. Each piece of clothing is worth one chip. A sock is worth a chip. So is a shoe."

One of the old people began to sneak inside the house. "No, you don't," the president shouted. "You must play with the clothes you have on. You can't sneak inside and put on a heap of clothes."

"This isn't fair," one sailor yelled. "Fuzz always wears three pairs of socks. That isn't fair."

[1]

"What do you mean it isn't fair?" Fuzz said, "I can't help it if I got jungle sickness. It was in the summer of twenty-three. We were near Wake Island when our ship—"

"Splat!" The president had thrown that pie. Several people picked Fuzz up and tossed him off the end of the dock.

"Let's begin the sale." The president snapped his fingers, and the con man came out with a large box. The president pointed to the box. "Here it is, ladies and gentlemen. Inside this box you might find a treasure or a turkey. It may be the wish of your dreams or a nightmare. What am I bid for this box and everything inside it?"

[1]

"Wait a minute," Thin Jim yelled. "How can we bid if we can't see what's in the box?"

"My good man," the president said, "if you don't wish to join in this sale, just step to the back of the crowd and give your three chips to your friends. But if you choose to stay and bid, you won't know what's inside a box until it is opened."

"Come on, give me your chips," said a woman next to Jim.

"Get out of here," Jim said. "I'm staying and I'm bidding. I bid one chip."

"Two chips," yelled Stan, the man who had dropped the first egg.

[1]

The president began to call, "I've got a bid for two, two, two, and who'll make it three, three, three? Who'll make it a three?"

"Three," the rancher yelled.

"Four," yelled Stan. He was sitting down, taking off his shoe.

The president called, "He's got a four, four, four. Who's going for a five, five, five? That's it. All done. Sold to the man for four. Get them in; get them out. Let's go."

The con man ran over to Stan, handed him the box, and picked up three chips and one shoe. Everybody crowded around as Stan opened the box. He reached inside and held up a baseball mitt.

"That's just what I need," he said. He sat down and put the mitt on his foot. "And to think I gave up a good shoe for this," he said.

[1]

The next box on sale went for three chips. Inside was a ticket that was good for twelve flying lessons. The next box went for five—two shoes, two socks, and one belt. Inside were two tickets to a baseball game.

The sailor who got that box was very mad. "And to think I gave up my clothes for two lousy baseball tickets," the sailor yelled.

Then the con man dragged out a box that was almost as big as he was. The bidding started. The rancher took off both her shoes and socks and her hat. "I'll bid eight," Emma said.

Thin Jim bid nine—three chips, two shoes, two socks, one shirt, and one belt.

Someone in the back yelled, "I bid ten."

[1]

1

A	B	C	D
ten	bubble	teeth	gasped
ton	babble	tooth	grasped

2

undershorts   around   float   hooray
watermelon   hollered   turtle   shirt

3

howling   laughter   comic   false   lovely
listening   magician   invisible   experiment
pillow   fingers   choke   lungs   mirror

4

The End

"I bid ten," Fuzz yelled, holding up three chips, a shoe, and his three pairs of socks.

Everyone around him was howling and cheering. "Going, going," the president yelled. "Gone to the man in the back."

Fuzz ran up and grabbed the box. He ripped it open. Inside was a comic book and sixty sticks of bubble gum.

"I can't chew this," Fuzz yelled. "It pulls out my false teeth." He passed the bubble gum around to the other people. They were blowing bubbles and getting gum all over their faces.

"That ends the sale," the president said. "But there is one last event, this—"

"Splat!" That was the last of the cream pies.

[1]

"This kind of horsing around will have to stop," the president yelled.

Nobody was listening to him. They were watching Pete. He was blowing a bubble as big as a watermelon. Then somebody broke it. Pete had a mask of gum.

"Our final event," the president said, "is Irma the Fantastic."

Everybody clapped. Someone said, "Who's that?"

"Don't you know?" a sailor said. "She's the most fantastic magician in the world."

"Where is she?" a man yelled.

"She's standing right next to me," the president said.

"She isn't, either," the man yelled.

[1]

Just then, one of the socks that had been bid in the sale began to float in the air. Then it seemed to slide onto a foot. The other sock floated onto another foot. Then a pair of pants seemed to slide onto an invisible body. Then a shirt went on the invisible body.

Now the whole body was visible, except for the head and the hands. The body walked toward the rancher. Slowly an invisible hand took the rancher's hat and placed it on the invisible head.

One man shouted, "Do you see what I see?"

The people clapped and yelled. Irma slowly took off the clothes. Then she rubbed some oil on her face. As she rubbed her face, it slowly became visible. All anyone could see was a face floating in the air.

[1]

Irma said, "I'm going to do a trick I've never done before. I'm going to make somebody else invisible. Since it's Salt's birthday, I'm going to experiment on him. I sure hope it works."

Everyone laughed and began to push Salt toward Irma. "Get your hands off me," Salt hollered.

Irma looked at Salt and frowned. "Since this is the first time I've made anybody else invisible, I don't think I'll make every part of him invisible. I think I'll just do half of his face."

[1]

She held a bit of invisible paint in her hand. She rubbed her hand up and down over the right half of Salt's face. As she rubbed, she said, "Oh, powers of powers, make his face invisible."

Then she stopped and shook her head. "I'm glad I didn't try this trick in my act," she said. "As you can see, it isn't working. Thank you anyhow, Salt. It looks like you're just not the invisible type."

"I never did trust magicians," Salt said.

Irma said, "But maybe you can help me with another trick." She handed him a pillow case. "Would you put this all the way over your head?"

"No, I don't—"

[1]

Before Salt could say anything more, Herman was helping Salt put the case over his head. Irma said to the people, "For my next trick, I'm going to change Salt into a lovely turtle. When I snap my fingers, he will become a little green turtle."

"I will not," Salt said. He jerked the pillow case from his head.

Half of his face was invisible. Everybody gasped and went, "Ohhh."

Irma handed Salt a mirror. Salt stared into the mirror. He started to say something, but he stopped. He just stared.

[1]

Irma said, "Oh, my. I didn't think it would work." Everybody except Salt laughed. Irma said, "I just wish I could remember how to make him visible."

Finally Irma came over with an oil rag and wiped his face. Slowly it became visible.

"I never did trust magicians," Salt said. "But glad I am that you made my face visible again."

Tony, Rosa, Salt, and everybody else had a big dinner. Then they sat around a large fire outside and sang old songs of the sea. And then it was time for Salt, Tony, and Rosa to go.

Suddenly all the people stopped joking around. Everything was quiet, except for the sound of logs on the fire.

[1]

Then Thin Jim said, "We all want to thank you, Salt. It's your birthday, but we're the ones who had the party. We used to be a bunch of old people, just sitting around here. But you showed us that we can still laugh and have a good time. We've got a lot of fun left in us. We—"

Thin Jim began to choke. He had tears in his eyes.

Someone yelled, "Let's hear it for Salt. Hip, hip, hooray! Hip, hip, hooray! Hip, hip, hooray!"

Tony never forgot the sound of those people yelling, "Hip, hip, hooray," at the top of their lungs. He never forgot the look of joy in their eyes. At one time he had thought that old people were funny, but he didn't feel that way any more.

THIS IS THE VERY END.

[1]